Berthold Lubetkin

Berthold LUBETKIN

John Allan

Photography by
Morley von Sternberg

Foreword by
Richard Meier

MERRELL

I must first acknowledge my collaborator, Morley von Sternberg, whose enthusiastic response to my original proposal to do an 'image-led' book on Lubetkin to mark his centenary turned the project from an idea into a reality.

Appreciation is due to the owners and occupiers of Lubetkin's buildings for their generous co-operation in allowing us to photograph the properties illustrated in this book, and also to those others who have assisted as intermediaries in arranging access.

I should like to record my thanks to colleagues at Avanti Architects for their encouragement, especially to Vicky Braouzou for her help with image scans and Lynn Melvin for word-processing assistance. I also gratefully acknowledge the professionalism and commitment of the team at Merrell Publishers.

Finally, for their continuing and unconditional support I thank my wife, Julie, and sons, Campbell and Stewart, to whom I dedicate this book.

John Allan

Important note
The inclusion of photographs, addresses and other details of buildings in this book does not imply any rights of public access or photography.

First published 2002 by
Merrell Publishers Limited
42 Southwark Street
London SE1 1UN

Telephone + 44 (0)20 7403 2047
E-mail mail@merrellpublishers.com

Publisher Hugh Merrell
Editorial Director Julian Honer
Managing Editor Anthea Snow
Art Director Matthew Hervey
Production Manager Kate Ward
Editorial and Production Assistant Emily Sanders

Distributed in the USA by Rizzoli International Publications, Inc. through St Martin's Press, 175 Fifth Avenue, New York, NY 10010

British Library Cataloguing-in-Publication Data:
Allan, John, 1945–
Berthold Lubetkin
1.Lubetkin, Berthold, 1901– 2.Architecture, Modern – 20th century – England
I.Title II.Von Sternberg, Morley
720.9'2

ISBN 1 85894 171 7

Edited by Richard Dawes
Indexed by Hilary Bird
Designed by Kate Ward

Printed and bound in Great Britain by Butler & Tanner Limited, Frome, Somerset

Front jacket: Highpoint I, London, 1933–35
Back jacket: The Penthouse, Highpoint II, London, 1935–38
Frontispiece: Staircase, Bevin Court, London, 1946–54

CONTENTS

6   Foreword by Richard Meier

9   BERTHOLD LUBETKIN
His Life and Work

52   LUBETKIN TODAY
An Illustrated Survey of Works

140   Lost Works

142   Select Bibliography

144   Index

FOREWORD

There is little question that Berthold Lubetkin is pre-eminent among architects of the Modern Movement in Britain. As John Allan has pointed out, his architecture could be characterized as "a unique fusion of intuition, intellect and idealism". Certainly Highpoint I in Highgate, north London, which is of exceptional stature as a canonical work of British modern architecture, is the best example of this talent and was at the time of its completion in 1935 a major triumph for modern architecture in England.

Through his work with Tecton, the group of architectural students that he brought together as a practice in 1932, and through his writing, Lubetkin spoke out for clarity, consistency and individual responsibility. His work, although occasionally baroque, like the Penguin Pool at London Zoo, shows the importance of imposing order on the whole process of building, from design to site. He believed passionately in modern architecture, rejecting the fashionable '–isms' as fragmented stances. These are values and convictions that I share and aspire to. Many of those whom he admired, such as Cervantes, Voltaire, Flaubert, Goethe and Freud, would have admired him as we do today.

For me, architecture is the form of light. Architecture is the physical manifestation of an idea of human experience. Architecture is the realization of coming together in a presence of light. It is expressed by form and seen through nature. Architecture is an idea of spatial organization by which man has realized his relationship between here and there, between now and then, between you and me, between what was and what can be.

As I have said before, architecture is an art of substance. It is the materialization of ideas about space. Given the demands of programme, site, locale and building technology, the architect endeavours to make buildings communicate in the language of materials and textures. Architecture is for the contemplation of the eyes and the mind, but, no less importantly, it is to be experienced and savoured by all human senses, and synthesized by the mind. You cannot have form in architecture that is unrelated to human experience, and one cannot approach an understanding of experience, in terms of architecture, without a strongly sensuous and tactile attitude towards form and space.

It seems to me that these ideas about the making of architecture also relate to the work of a number of other architects of Lubetkin's generation, architects whose work I have admired and learned from – architects such as Le Corbusier, Theo van Doesburg and J.J.P. Oud, all of whom visited Highpoint I shortly after its completion and praised it as a work of exceptional importance, as well as Mies van der Rohe, Alvar Aalto and, later, James Stirling, to name but a few. Each expressed his vision in a different way, and for each, as with Berthold Lubetkin, there was a search for harmony, a rational procedure, a precision of detail, constructional integrity, a respect for human scale, and, most importantly, "the expression of faith in ideology … and the creation of architecture that contained a message for the future".

The Penguin Pool, London Zoo, 1934.

Richard Meier, January 2002

"We wanted to give a face to our age." Thus Berthold Lubetkin in old age [1] summed up the aim of his contemporaries, a generation of architects who believed that the emerging modern world of the twentieth century demanded a radical new architecture to serve its needs and express its hopes. In England in the 1930s and for a further period after the Second World War, nobody realized this ambition more purposefully or poetically than Lubetkin himself. Indeed, it is largely on account of the work he accomplished in that decade, while not yet forty years old, that he has been variously described as having "as good a claim as any to being regarded the greatest architect in Britain of the century" and as her "one master of unimpeachable world standing". The optimism and sense of order embodied in his buildings continue to inspire those who see or use them, and the fact that most of his surviving work is now listed – twenty-five buildings, including five at Grade I – surely confirms that his contribution reveals an authentic face of its age.

Lubetkin's meteoric career combined triumph and rejection, like that of the great Swiss architect Le Corbusier, to whom he is sometimes compared. Although Lubetkin was fourteen years younger, and thus a second-generation Modernist, like Le Corbusier he both personified the Modern Movement and was one of its most far-sighted critics. His work exemplifies its key precepts: the vision of architecture as an instrument of social progress, the beneficial use of technology and the pursuit of a radical aesthetic. But Lubetkin was no Functionalist and was much too intelligent to follow a party line. His warnings of modern architecture's increasing anonymity, its disregard of history and loss of human resonance began thirty years before the onset of widespread public alienation in the 1960s and 1970s. His own work is deeply personal, densely coded and visually rich, and confounds the notion that 'complexity and contradiction' were innovative concepts of a succeeding generation that the modern tradition could not accommodate. The powerful geometrical discipline so characteristic of his design is invariably shot through or lightened with lyrical contrasts to produce a balance of opposites, which he would expound in philosophical terms as a representation of the mutuality of mind and matter, or the interdependence of reason and emotion, science and art – none of which could explain the world on its own. His socialist conviction was firmly, if undogmatically, grounded in Marxist theory, which underpinned but did not inhibit his understanding of architecture as a practical discipline. Rather, his belief in the reciprocal influence of architecture and social practice was his primary professional motivation. While his direct experience of the ideological struggles and setbacks in revolutionary Russia made him sceptical of current theories of determinism and the *Zeitgeist*, he never doubted the transforming potential of architecture and believed passionately in the capacity of buildings to communicate a social message, albeit in microcosm and through metaphor. His artistic sources ranged far and wide in geography and history, yet his poetic sensibilities coexisted with an abiding concern for practical details and human needs. Indeed, the commitment he lavished on their considerate solution and clear presentation raised this seemingly mundane aspect of an architect's duties to a didactic level and is itself an expression of his philosophical ideals.

1. Berthold Lubetkin, photographed in 1985.

Lubetkin was charismatic but elusive, captivating and humorous in company but a fearsome opponent in argument, with formidable intellectual range. His exotic background and foreigner's English only thinly masked a penetrating grasp of British culture and social convention. For a generation of architects in the 1930s he was their guiding light, and in those who worked with him he inspired devoted loyalty and lifelong respect. For others he remained an enigma, and he infuriated and baffled his critics. In the 1980s, fifty years after his best-known buildings were completed, he reappeared from obscurity to become a cult figure for a new generation of students and young people who found in his work and social commentary a sanity and seriousness to set against the sterile trivialities of the day.

Like any truly creative figure, Lubetkin defies simple historical categorization. His ideas and his built legacy lie at the heart of the Modern Movement. But they could also be seen to contain timeless and universal messages, and still present a challenge to contemporary assumptions about architecture and city building. He was of his time yet in a class of his own, but one thing is certain: to appreciate the history of modern British architecture and gain a perspective on its current context, you have to grapple with Lubetkin and engage with his extraordinary story.

Berthold Lubetkin's origins are remote and uncertain. He is believed to have been born on 14 December 1901 in Tiflis (Tbilisi), in Georgia, the only son of Fenya (Hassya) Minim and Roman (Rubin) Aronovich Lubetkin, a small businessman who imported control equipment and ticketing machinery for the armed forces and state transport industry. Like many details of Berthold Lubetkin's early life, however, even his date of birth is unconfirmed by documentary evidence. His British passport recorded his date and place of birth as 1903, Warsaw, an apparent contradiction explained by Lubetkin as an expedient fiction to eliminate a period of cadet service in the Red Army that might have obstructed his early student movements around Europe. What is certain is that his formative years in Russia and the coincidence of his coming of age with the convulsive upheaval of the Revolution of 1917 were crucial in the development of his political outlook and artistic vocation.

The family was of Jewish origin, moderately prosperous and well travelled, so that by 1914 Lubetkin had already visited France, Germany, England and Scandinavia. He would also accompany his father on business trips within Russia. His cultural range and precocious gift for languages can surely be traced to these early cosmopolitan experiences. He was educated at the Tenishevskaya Gymnasium in St Petersburg and the Medvednikov Gymnasium in Moscow, both, in his own words, "bastions of orthodoxy" that, in retrospect, would seem quaintly at odds with what was to follow. More enduring in the formation of his architectural sensibilities was the civic grandeur of St Petersburg itself, with its spatial axes and urban drama – qualities he would seek to reinterpret in a modern idiom many years later.

Lubetkin's first-hand experience of the Revolution marked him for life. His recollections of the momentous events of 1917 and the immediate aftermath [2], when he was living in the centre of Moscow, remained vivid into old age. But out of the kaleidoscope of activity, personalities and excitement a central theme

2. Third Anniversary of the Revolution, Petrograd (now St Petersburg), 1920 – a mass theatrical re-enactment at which Lubetkin was present.

emerged that would underpin his maturing outlook and professional philosophy: a profound belief in the linkage of art and social practice, and the capacity, indeed duty, of architecture to project and exemplify the promise of an oncoming better world. Though the subsequent development of Stalin's Soviet Union left him as dismayed and disillusioned as any Western critic, the imprint of that initial moment of hope, with its seemingly unlimited sense of possibility and purpose, never left him.

It is thought that Lubetkin's artistic education began with his enrolment at the Stroganov Art School in Moscow on the eve of the Revolution. But this institution, like many others, was rapidly transformed, with the result that his studies were transferred to the SVOMAS (Free Art) Studios and the Vkhutemas (Higher State Artistic and Technical Workshops) in St Petersburg and Moscow. It is clear, however, that the training he received bore scant resemblance to any sort of curriculum or architectural course as these might nowadays be conventionally understood. It was, at least initially, a period of improvisation and experiment, using any resources that came to hand, and one in which, by his own recollection, the very concept of certificates or diplomas was anathema by reason of its association with the former academic regime. "We were simply inventors," he recalled, "anything else would have been a betrayal of the artist's revolutionary mission."

This avid search also led to Lubetkin's participation in several radical groups, including Proletcult and ASNOVA, where the rôle of revolutionary art and architecture in the development of the Revolution was the prime subject of debate. Yet immersed in this ideological ferment as he became, he was careful to point out that his own contribution was as nothing compared to what he absorbed in listening to and meeting such leading figures of the Constructivist period as Rodchenko, Tatlin, Malevich, Mayakovsky, Vesnin, Popova and Gabo. With such rare teachers and high expectations, it is not surprising that when he left Russia in 1922 the experiences of these formative years had fuelled him with a creative energy that would last a lifetime.

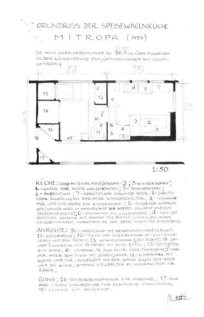

Examples of Lubetkin's student work:

3. Early dwelling model project, c. 1921.

4. 'Mitropa', a detailed dimensional study of a railway carriage, 1929.

It would be quite wrong to see Lubetkin's departure at this moment as a political defection, and although the waning of that initial phase of 'heroic communism' signalled that the regime and the times were changing, his move was essentially motivated by the desire to develop. Five years on from the heady days of 1917, with the Soviet Union still weakened by civil war, famines and foreign threats, Lubetkin now realized that he must look further afield to equip himself with the technical knowledge and professional experience necessary to turn the brave slogans of the Revolution into real and useful architecture. Obtaining a rôle as translator allowed him to go to Berlin in 1922 with the *First Exhibition of Russian Art*, a pioneering cultural offensive to reveal the work of the revolutionary avant-garde to a wider European audience. When the exhibition later transferred to Amsterdam, however, it left Lubetkin, who spoke no Dutch, looking for a way to further his studies.

Feeling that the Bauhaus had little to offer beyond what his Russian artistic experiments had already given him, he remained in Berlin and enrolled at the Bauschule at the Technische Hochschule in Charlottenburg and the Höhere Fachschule für Textil und Bekleidungsindustrie. Learning simultaneously the theory and practice of concrete and carpet-making might seem a bizarre combination of pursuits but it is entirely characteristic of Lubetkin, an instinctual autodidact, to have assembled the desired elements of his own education in this way. In fact, both these fields of knowledge were to play vital rôles in his eventual architectural practice.

Still Lubetkin, the self-styled "rootless journeyman", remained mobile, and, after gaining a short travel scholarship in 1923 to study the carpet collections in Vienna, he moved to Poland, where, supported by his father's branch office, he took a diploma in architecture at the Warsaw Polytechnic [5]. This was as close to a conventional regime of study as he ever experienced, but such was his mastery of the subject-matter that he compressed the usual three years' coursework into little over half that time and promptly resumed his travels.

5. Lubetkin pictured c. 1923, when he entered Warsaw Polytechnic.

In 1925 Lubetkin moved to Paris, then at its zenith as the artistic capital of Europe, and over the next six years made the crucial transition from precocious student to proven practitioner. His arrival coincided with the huge and influential Exposition Internationale des Arts Décoratifs et Industriels Modernes, where he assisted in the construction of the Soviet Pavilion and related kiosks by Konstantin Melnikov and first met Le Corbusier, whose own Pavillon de l'Esprit Nouveau was being built near by. Though Lubetkin described this encounter in anecdotal rather than revelatory terms, it marked the beginning of a professional journey that would take him from adulation of the Swiss master to critical opposition.

With the Exposition over, Lubetkin again sought out the necessary elements of his professional education by enrolling at four separate institutions in Paris: the Ecole Spéciale d'Architecture, the Institut d'Urbanisme, the Ecole Supérieure de Béton Armé (which specialized in reinforced concrete) and the Ecole des Beaux-Arts. To the daunting array of options that these offered he rapidly applied his confident selectivity, taking only what he felt was of value, whether or not it represented a unit of study or conferred a certificate. And of all these experiences it was from the Ecole des Beaux-Arts – or, more precisely, the independent atelier of Auguste Perret, which had split from the Ecole – that Lubetkin gained most. Having just completed the celebrated modern church of Notre Dame at Le Raincy, east of Paris, Perret was the doyen of the French profession and its foremost exponent of reinforced-concrete architecture. But he was also a former Beaux-Arts man, a classicist and a living link with the nineteenth-century tradition of structural rationalism. Lubetkin's brief period of tutelage, which he acknowledged as an enduring debt, implanted in him the vital insight that the human resonance and compositional discipline of classicism could continue to inform modern architecture despite the obsolescence of the literal classical vocabulary. This understanding of classicism not as a style but as a source of order and precision imparting a certain sense of ceremony was to become a defining theme of Lubetkin's mature work.

Alongside these fragmentary studies a more informal, though no less significant, process of education was in train. This was simply Lubetkin's experience of living in Paris itself, in the café culture of Montparnasse, amid the dazzling array of ideas and personalities that continued to illuminate his travels. A list of his encounters from Berlin to Paris – with Paul Klee and George Grosz, Thomas and Heinrich Mann, Schoenberg and Hindemith, Picasso and Braque, Léger, Gris, Soutine, Cocteau, Ernst May, Bruno Taut, Käthe Kollwitz – reads like a roll-call of key figures in early twentieth-century radical culture.

But the Bohemian lifestyle of the Left Bank was an impecunious one, and Lubetkin's quest for education and ideas was rapidly overlaid by the need to support himself. One rewarding enterprise was the production of surrogate diploma schemes for wealthier but less energetic finalists at the Ecole Spéciale [6]. A miscellany of small design commissions and flat conversions also yielded intermittent subsistence income [7], while the nightclub project Le Trapèze Volant, for a troupe of circus acrobats, was a more unusual, but one-off, opportunity [8]. With characteristic

6. A new airport for Paris: one of Lubetkin's surrogate diploma projects, c. 1927–30.

initiative, and following up his previous work as a translator, Lubetkin obtained a position with the USSR Trades Delegation in France. His task was to curate a travelling exhibition of Soviet goods and imports in a demountable timber pavilion that he designed in collaboration with the architect J. Volodko [9]. This promotional programme, which extended over three years from the late 1920s, took Lubetkin to various sites in France and provided further useful experience in construction and the logistics of exhibition installation.

By now, with some seven years of travel and study under his belt, Lubetkin was impatient to tackle his first major building and test his mastery of the new toolbox of modern architecture. Providentially, an ideal opportunity appeared. The project was an apartment block in the avenue de Versailles, Paris, which Lubetkin undertook in association with Jean Ginsberg, a contemporary from Warsaw who had also attended the Ecole Spéciale and whose father formed the Société Civile l'Habitation Contemporaine – the development company that financed the project.

Number 25, avenue de Versailles is an eight-storey infill block in an existing street frontage with a difficult north–west orientation [11]. The plan comprises a two-bedroom flat on the main façade with a studio unit at the rear and an ingenious light well indirectly illuminating the otherwise buried staircase. The two young architects had clearly mastered the Corbusian essentials of *pilotis*, strip windows, frame structure and roof garden, albeit within the constraints of the site and onerous local regulations that dictated closely negotiated setbacks at ground and roof levels [10]. The structure combined a reinforced-concrete frame with hollow pot floors and rendered façades, the current progressive convention, but there is nothing tentative or derivative here. The scale and assurance of the scheme matched anything Le Corbusier had so far built. Take the windows, for example: set in crisply modelled reveals and prudently weathered with deep sills, these are purpose-designed vertical sliding sashes that retract fully into a spandrel cavity with a fold-over sill detail, virtually turning the living-room into an open balcony. The organization of services, the specification of fittings and finishes, and the elegant resolution of details and

(Opposite, clockwise from top left)

7. Apartment conversion project, 31, rue de l'Université, Paris, c. 1927.

8. Club Trapèze Volant, Paris, 1927.

9. USSR Trades Exhibition Pavilion, typical view of interior installation, 1929.

10. 25, avenue de Versailles, Paris: the roof terrace, designed as an outdoor gymnasium.

11. 25, avenue de Versailles by Lubetkin and J. Ginsberg, 1928–31.

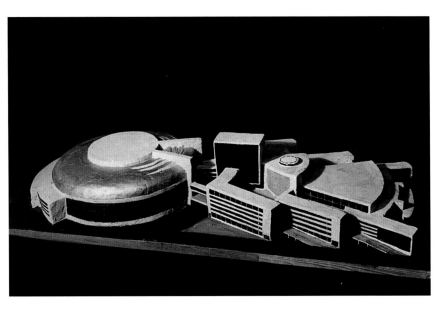

junctions likewise all speak of independent and confident technical judgement [12]. Completed in 1931, when both designers were still under thirty, this extraordinarily assured and widely reported work announced Lubetkin's arrival on the modern architectural stage.

The association with Ginsberg having run its course, Lubetkin now faced the question of how and where to direct his proven skills and intense professional ambition. His original plan had been to return to the Soviet Union and take his place in building the new social order, but the prospects had clouded since the time of his departure. Throughout his period of European travel in the 1920s Lubetkin had maintained contact with developments and former comrades in the Soviet Union, and also remained engaged with Soviet architectural discourse by entering local competitions. In the most important of these, for the Palace of Soviets in Moscow, Lubetkin's entry, submitted in 1931 with colleagues Sigalin and Blum, gained a cash prize. But it also proved to be a turning-point.

The competition to design the Palace of Soviets was a major international event that attracted entrants from all over the world, including modern masters such as Le Corbusier, Perret, Walter Gropius, Erich Mendelsohn and Hans Poelzig. Lubetkin's entry illustrates his rare skill in the systematic organization of a daunting brief [13]. This called for two huge auditoria to seat fifteen thousand and six thousand delegates respectively, extensive office accommodation and a vast library. The plan is a clear fusion of the two strands of his architectural training and early experience – the dynamic Constructivist influences from the Soviet Union and the classical rationalism derived from his studies in Paris. It is certainly not difficult to see already the strong geometrical discipline that was to become a consistent theme of Lubetkin's mature practice.

Yet although the competition brought personal success for Lubetkin, its eventual outcome – reworking the entry of Soviet architect Boris Iofan into a crude exercise in Stalinist propaganda – revealed the retrogression of Soviet architecture

12. 25, avenue de Versailles: view of an apartment living-room, showing fitted furniture.

13. Competition project for the Palace of Soviets, by Lubetkin with G. Sigalin and Blum, 1931.

under the new regime. This dismal prospect, added to disturbing stories of friends' disappearance back home, caused Lubetkin to rethink his situation. Where did circumstances now place him – the committed socialist who ardently wished to pursue the radical possibilities of Modernism?

Lubetkin had already made a couple of exploratory trips to England at the request of the Soviet Trade Delegation to recommend potential entrants for the Palace of Soviets competition. But a fortuitous meeting in Paris of his companion Prascovia Schuberski with her former Cambridge flatmate Margaret Gardiner led to his being invited to design a substantial house in Hampstead, north London. Though this commission, from Ralph and Manya Harari, never came to fruition, it was sufficient to suggest the prospect of a professional future in England, which he visited again in late 1931, when he was immediately taken up by the progressive architectural and intellectual establishment. Within weeks he had met Hubert de Cronin Hastings, editor of the *Architectural Review*, Sir Ian MacAlister, secretary of the Royal Institute of British Architects, Charles Reilly, Professor of the Liverpool School of Architecture and a range of leading figures, including J.D. Bernal and George Bernard Shaw, as well as receiving invitations to the Architecture Club, the Art Workers' Guild and the Architectural Association.

The speed and ease of this reception is as much an indication of Lubetkin's social resourcefulness as of his appeal to a select English audience as an exotic foreigner, personable, charismatic, with first-hand experience of the huge events in Europe of the previous decade.For his part, Lubetkin was attracted by British traditions of tolerance and scientific progress, and by the possibility of making his own mark in a country where continental modern architecture had yet to arrive. Moreover, remembering such slogans as "Homes for Heroes", he was also led to expect that there would be real opportunities for social building. He later acknowledged that these initial optimistic assumptions were a touch naïve, being coloured by the warmth of the welcome and the prospect of immediate work. But in any case the alternatives were no more promising.

In 1932, with six graduates of the Architectural Association, Lubetkin formed the Tecton partnership and set up practice in Gower Street, London. Godfrey Samuel, son of the Liberal Party's Deputy Leader, Sir Herbert (later Lord) Samuel, Michael Dugdale and Valentine Harding had already been to Oxford, while Anthony Chitty had previously studied architecture at Trinity College, Cambridge. Francis Skinner and Lindsay Drake were slightly younger and had entered the AA directly from school [14]. All had shared a disenchantment with its traditional teaching programme and had visited, or were aware of, progressive developments in Europe. The adoption of a collective title, partly to signify the teamwork ideal, partly for mere convenience, was unprecedented and was certainly not favourably regarded by the professional establishment. But although nominally a group of equals, Tecton was dominated by Lubetkin, with his rich European experience, mercurial personality and clear sense of artistic direction. This pre-eminent position also characterized the firm's working method, whereby design initiation and direction became Lubetkin's

14. Tecton group, c. 1938. Left to right: Francis Skinner, Eileen Murray, Margaret Church, Denys Lasdun, Lubetkin, Carl Ludwig Franck and Lindsay Drake.

exclusive prerogative, with the other partners and architectural assistants effectively serving as a research, development and delivery team – a powerful symbiosis that joined Lubetkin's creative imagination with his colleagues' conscientious productivity.

At one level it is legitimate to see Lubetkin's assimilation as part of the larger pattern of relocation already occurring in the early 1930s. The ensuing years would see a gathering stream of émigrés and refugees from Europe and elsewhere, with the result that the artistic and cultural scene in England became characterized by its cosmopolitan cast list. By mid-decade this was to include Gropius, Marcel Breuer, Mendelsohn, László Moholy-Nagy, Arthur Korn and Ernö Goldfinger, to name but a few. Meanwhile, from Canada came Wells Coates, Fred Lasserre and Christopher Tunnard, and, from New Zealand, Amyas Connell and Basil Ward. The local partnerships that blossomed from this influx are also significant: Gropius and Maxwell Fry, Breuer and F.R.S. Yorke, Mendelsohn and the Russian-born but English-bred Serge Chermayeff. Other arrivals, such as Carl Ludwig Franck and Peter Moro, were taken in by Lubetkin himself.

It would be wrong, however, to read too much homogeneity into this redeployment. Motives, backgrounds, skills and outlooks differed considerably, and many of the figures referred to above were temporary residents and moved on to the United States or elsewhere. In Lubetkin's case, the apparent ease of his professional relocation in England is deceptive. He himself recalled his uncertainty over its permanence, continuing for several years to hang on to the possibility of returning to the Soviet Union. He revisited his homeland on at least two further occasions before 1935, once specifically to consider employment at Makeyevka in the Don Basin, and surviving correspondence with Russian relatives reveals continuing ambivalence over his long-term plans. His settling in England is better understood less as a large or single ideologically motivated decision than as the eventual result of an initial opportunity that rapidly led to a degree of professional involvement and recognition from which it became unrealistic to disengage. Yet even to this explanation must be added the unquantifiable factor of his preferred stance as 'outsider', the sense of never quite being part of his context. In this respect England perhaps suited him perfectly: he could feel simultaneously welcome and independent, engaged but able to work on his own terms. Indeed, this extended to his relationship with Tecton, which did not exclude an opportune association with A.V. Pilichowski for his first English housing commission.

The fact that several of the other partners in Tecton also supplemented their income by occasional work outside the firm indicates the difficulties facing young architects at the time. With the building industry still suffering from the Depression, the economic outlook in Britain was far from encouraging for a fledgeling practice in search of clients and commissions to match its radical aspirations. Public-sector or prestige projects were securely in the hands of establishment firms, and even individual private houses, the most likely début project for a young professional, were largely the province of well-connected practitioners. But given the contacts available to Godfrey Samuel through his father, Tecton did have an unusual

15. The Gorilla House, London Zoo, 1933, Lubetkin's first building in Britain.

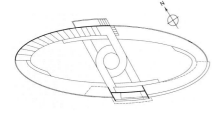

16. Plan of the Penguin Pool, London Zoo, 1934, described by Lubetkin as "a purely geometric mathematical shape within which all sorts of fantasies were possible".

advantage. It was Samuel's introductions to senior staff at London Zoo, the Gestetner family and, indirectly, the leaders of Finsbury Borough Council that were to provide Lubetkin and his colleagues with all their principal sources of work.

Tecton's prime years of practice were from 1932 to the outbreak of the Second World War, and its output can be grouped into four categories: the zoo work, a variety of individual houses, the famous Highpoint apartments in north London and the work for Finsbury Borough Council, the last of which bridged the war years and continued to sustain the firm until its dissolution in 1948.

The first category comprises the remarkable series of zoological commissions. This improbable genre of modern architecture developed from Godfrey Samuel's contact with Solly Zuckerman, a research anatomist at London Zoo, through whom Lubetkin was introduced to its Superintendent, Geoffrey Vevers, and secretary, Sir Peter Chalmers Mitchell, both of whom were immediately captivated by his ideas and energy, and who were, like him, fervent socialists. A steady stream of commissions ensued, starting with the Gorilla House in 1933 [15], an ingenious circular design in reinforced concrete with revolving screens and retractable roof, and leading to one of Tecton's best-known works, the Penguin Pool at Regent's Park, completed in 1934 [16, 17]. This tiny structure brought Lubetkin international celebrity and represents many of his preoccupations, albeit in miniature: the diametric geometrical organization and sculptural form, a certain theatricality and a distinct sense of humour. Its technical virtuosity, accomplished with the help of the Danish engineer Ove Arup, lies not only in the audacious structural mechanics of the famous ramps (calculated, according to legend, over a weekend by Arup's assistant Felix Samuely), but also in the way the massive concrete abutments that actually support them are concealed within elements of the perimeter.

This association of Lubetkin and Arup, the foremost exponents of their respective crafts in England at the time, must be recognized as one of the most fruitful

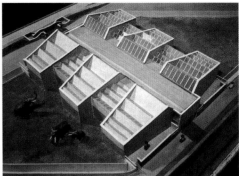

23. Studio of Animal Art, London Zoo, 1936–37, later demolished.

(Opposite, clockwise from top left)

17. The Penguin Pool, London Zoo, 1934, seen here in 1987 after refurbishment.

18. Unbuilt project for a new Elephant and Rhino Pavilion, London Zoo, 1937–39.

19. The Polar Bear Pit, Dudley Zoo, 1935–37.

20. Detail of the Entrance, Dudley Zoo, 1935–37.

21. The Elephant House, Whipsnade Zoo, 1935, in its original setting.

22. The Entrance Shelter and Kiosk, Whipsnade Zoo, 1934.

collaborations of the Modern Movement. Yet merely to acknowledge its creativity and idealism would be to overlook a more subtle but no less vital characteristic – their shared conviction that, contrary to naïve Functionalist precepts of 'structural honesty', structure should be expressed when it was architecturally significant and suppressed when it was not. Further projects at Regent's Park were to follow, including a Studio of Animal Art [23], a new North Gatehouse and a substantial project for a new Elephant and Rhino Pavilion [18], which was halted at the outbreak of war.

Tecton also undertook work for the same client at Whipsnade Zoo, a large country park just north of London opened in 1931. Several projects were achieved, including giraffe and elephant exhibits, an entrance building [22] and the visitors' restaurant. The most substantial of these was the Elephant House of 1935, which provides a transparent statement of Lubetkin's classical sensibilities – the symmetrical organization of simple Platonic solids, the laconic expression and the heightened contrast between abstract form and a pastoral landscape [21]. As he once put it, the aim of the zoo work was to present "a vision of nature tamed, not with a fist but with a smile".

These themes found their most comprehensive application at Dudley Zoo, just outside Birmingham, which Tecton designed on a virgin site and completed in just eighteen months. Here a whole ensemble of animal and social pavilions was planned in the steep and thickly wooded surroundings of Dudley Castle, a scheduled Ancient Monument dating from the eleventh century. The scheme shows considerable ingenuity in the introduction of buildings of uncompromisingly modern design into a sensitive context [19, 20]. Moreover, by virtue of their consistent geometric character, a sort of family kinship is established between the buildings, twelve of which still remain [24], despite their widely differing functions. Accounts of the zoo's opening in 1937, attracting some 250,000 visitors, indicate the spectacular popular success of the project. Indeed, it may be that more of the British public first

24. View at Dudley with the Aviary (top), part of the Bear Ravine (left) and a kiosk (right), showing the geometric consistency used to link the structures in the landscape.

(Opposite, clockwise from top left)

25. Terraced housing at Greenwich, London, by Lubetkin and A.V. Pilichowski, 1933–34

26. The Beach House, Aldwick Bay, West Sussex, 1933–34.

27. Lubetkin's 'dacha', Hillfield ('Bungalow A'), Whipsnade, 1933–36.

28. Holly Frindle ('Bungalow B'), Whipsnade, 1933–36, showing frame-and-panel wall system and the shadow-gap plinth detail.

encountered modern architecture through Lubetkin's 1930s zoo work than by any other means.

The second category of works consists of individual houses, although Tecton's success in finding other and larger commissions perhaps renders these less significant in the practice's overall output than would be the case for most of their Modernist contemporaries. Those from Lubetkin's own hand are nonetheless of distinctive identity. Two were speculative projects, and in this respect, if not stylistically, may be linked with the huge development of the popular house market in the interwar years. The scheme of four three-storey houses in Greenwich, south-east London, is particularly unusual, perhaps even unique, within the 1930s Modernist canon in adapting a traditional London type-form, the terraced house, to a modern idiom [25]. The single house at Aldwick Bay, on the Sussex coast, is more typical of the contemporary trend for seaside villas, though it still displays Lubetkin's characteristic symmetrical planning and lyrical composition [26].

The most evocative example of individual houses, however, is the bungalow that Lubetkin built for himself in 1935 as a weekend 'dacha' just outside Whipsnade Zoo [27]. Its response to the splendid setting was as instrumental as it was inspired, involving considerable earthworks to create a platform from which the building could command the sweeping view below. But in this and a second bungalow near by [28], Lubetkin also took the opportunity to explore several ideas used in his later work: the frame-and-panel walling system, the idea of the tapering corridor and the distinctive 'shadow gap' device that separates the building from the ground. This was the sort of detail that, for him, had both programmatic and philosophic

implications: programmatic in eliminating *piloti* where they were not justified yet still maintaining a clean lower edge to the elevation, uncompromised by the muddy tidemark below the traditional damp-proof course; philosophic in maintaining the classical abstraction of the design, the clarity of distinction between the man-made world and the natural world.

But Lubetkin had a more ambitious design concept for modern living than the single, or even the terraced, house. This was the modern flat. The ideal of the compactly planned, fully equipped collective apartment building had preoccupied architects and urbanists since before the turn of the century. More specifically, it had been a key theme throughout Lubetkin's formative years of study and travel, from Constructivist debates when he was still in the Soviet Union, through Germany, with its large housing experiments, and Paris, where Le Corbusier's Plan Voisin for a modern city of towers in parkland had been exhibited at the Exposition of 1925 and developed in his later publication *La Ville Radieuse*. Lubetkin and Ginsberg's apartment block in Paris had provided invaluable experience in the technical realization of a sizeable modern building, but the limitations of the site meant it could not serve as a generic example of progressive urban theory. With Samuel's introduction of Lubetkin to Sigmund Gestetner in 1932/33, the perfect opportunity arose for such a demonstration.

The apartment blocks at Highpoint [29] are perhaps the most celebrated of all Tecton's 1930s works, widely illustrated and the object of international acclaim both at the time and ever since. Le Corbusier, who, at Lubetkin's invitation, visited the project on completion, admitted that "for a long time he had dreamed of executing dwellings in such conditions for the good of humanity", describing Highpoint I as "an achievement of the first rank, and a milestone which will be useful to everybody".

Highpoint I, finished in 1935, is usually regarded as the principal work, but the two blocks should be seen as an ensemble in the context of their whole site [30]. This is not just because together they represent the scale of Tecton's essay in collective apartment living and its dependence on a large, fully landscaped estate, but also because the buildings themselves illustrate Lubetkin's stylistic development over the decade.

Gestetner, director of a large office-machinery company in north London, had originally intended to develop residential apartments for members of his workforce. However, following pre-letting promotion, market values quickly exceeded norms for low-cost housing and the units were largely appropriated as desirable middle-class flats.

Highpoint illustrates dramatically the Corbusian town-planning proposition, whereby the accommodation is concentrated into a densely planned structure and raised off the ground by *piloti* [31], thus releasing the maximum remaining area for communal facilities and recreational landscaping. Unlike so many later flawed attempts in the typical post-war municipal housing estate, this modern ideal really is achieved at Highpoint, where the gardens are beautifully planted

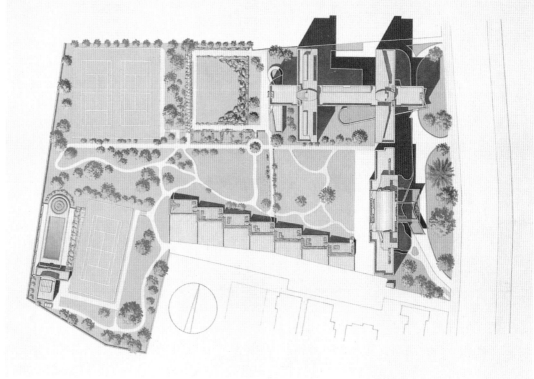

29. Highpoint I, 1933–35 (left), and Highpoint II, 1936–38 (right), north London, seen from the gardens.

30. The Highpoint site plan, showing the extent of landscaping with gardens, pathways, tennis courts and swimming-pool.

Key to plans

1. Hall and winter garden
2. Hall
3. Porter's flat
4. Large flat
5. Lifts and staircases
6. One-room flats
7. Tea-room
8. Maids' bedrooms
9. Entrance hall
10. Living-room
11. Dining-room
12. Bedroom
13. Kitchen
14. Bathroom
15. Service lift
16. Drying balcony

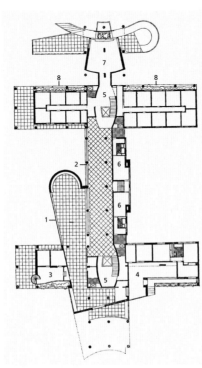

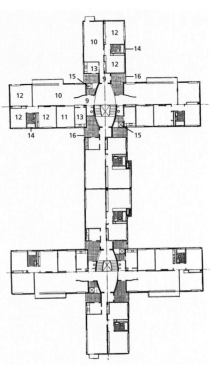

and maintained, and incorporate tennis courts, children's play areas, a squash court and a swimming-pool.

The ground floor is arranged freely around the grid of *piloti* that support the rectilinear carcass of accommodation above. The narrow site frontage dictated a longitudinal development, so with characteristic grace Lubetkin orientates the entrance on an oblique axis in order to bypass the first stair tower and arrive opposite the centre of the building [33]. This equalizes the significance of the two cores, which are, in fact, symmetrical in the upper-level plan [32]. The *promenade architecturale* continues at the far end of the hall [34] down to a tea-room, which leads to steps and an arabesque ramp into the gardens. Apart from its functional elegance, this ground-floor composition was also intended by Lubetkin as a lyrical abstraction to contrast with the repetitive order of the flats above. These are arranged in a double cruciform, four apartments radiating from each staircase, which ingeniously receives borrowed daylight from two diagonally opposite corners, the other two corners containing service lifts.

An advanced system of construction was devised by Ove Arup that avoided intrusive framing and used a system of climbing formwork that enabled the monolithic concrete carcass to be cast without conventional scaffolding [35]. The interior fitting-out is also full of consideration and innovation, with even the most mundane details subjected to rigorous reappraisal. The sliding folding windows used in the living-rooms are particularly ambitious, allowing the whole sash range to be folded and slid to the end of the window opening, turning the room into a virtual balcony – a variation of the retractable window design used in the Paris block. Everything from a bath lip to a door escutcheon was interrogated with the same rationalizing scrutiny. This discipline was powerfully demonstrated in the publication of a series of explanatory diagrams covering practically every detail, giving the whole work an exemplary didactic quality that certainly helped to secure its canonical status. Indeed, the promotional impact of Tecton's own self-presentation may itself have lent plausibility to the Functionalist cause, placing Lubetkin in a critical category to which he did not truly belong. The apartment interiors, for example, notwithstanding the pervasive rationality, happily accommodate a variety of tastes in décor and furniture that could be regarded as quite contrary to the architectural ethos of the building generally.

Highpoint I's pioneering reputation has always outshone its compromises: the ninety-degree overlooking of adjoining flats; the odd arrangement of service terminals, which made it necessary in some cases to enter a neighbour's flat in order to read the electric meter; poor acoustic and fire separation in the service lifts; and a high-maintenance envelope that has needed onerous repair over the succeeding years. Perhaps most significantly, from Lubetkin's point of view, the intention that foyer areas should function as a sort of social forum never came to fruition. Neither, for that matter, has the roof terrace – a key element in Le Corbusier's theory of modern building – ever been fully exploited, furnished or planted as originally intended.

34. The raised ground-floor landing at Highpoint I, with its diffuse lighting screen.

35. Highpoint I under construction, showing the climbing shuttering system and avoidance of scaffolding.

(Opposite, clockwise from top left)

31. The entrance at night, Highpoint I. "Highpoint stands on tiptoe and spreads its wings," wrote one observer.

32. Typical upper-floor plan, Highpoint I. The wings contain the larger, three-bed flats, with two-bed flats in the spine. The structural bisection of the plan avoids a corridor but necessitates bedroom access via living-rooms.

33. Ground-floor plan, Highpoint I. The angled foyer leads to a raised landing and the two stair-and-lift cores. A porter's flat, maids' rooms and a three-bed flat occupy the wings, and there are two studio flats in the spine.

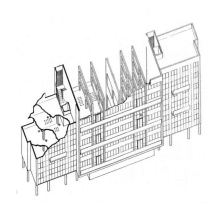

37. Cutaway study of Highpoint II's structure, showing monolithic wings and transverse-framed central section.

Nonetheless, Highpoint I has remained Lubetkin's single most acclaimed work, becoming so much the flagship of the British Modern Movement that he was to find it difficult to advance without critical dissent. It also projected the firm, through the plaudits of historian and critic Henry Russell Hitchcock, to an American audience, featuring prominently in the exhibition *Modern Architecture in England* at New York's Museum of Modern Art in 1937.

Highpoint II followed in 1938, after Gestetner had acquired the adjacent site to prevent an inappropriate development [36]. After intensive and at times absurd negotiations with the local planning authority, only a much smaller block was permitted, which, being on more expensive land, necessitated an even more luxurious design and specification in order to secure an adequate market return. Only twelve maisonettes are contained in the second block, as against the sixty flats of Highpoint I.

The lavish accommodation, beautifully planned [38], offered what was probably the most desirable and advanced apartment-living in England. The spiral staircases of the two central stacks of maisonettes rise through double-storey-height voids and give commanding views across the living space towards Hampstead Heath. The kitchens and bathrooms were meticulously fitted out, and even the lifts were specially customized to deliver visitors directly to the apartment with no communal landing.

The different dwelling programme of Highpoint II also produced an innovative structural solution, a hybrid of frame and monolithic external wall. This resulted in a composite architectural expression, the central framed portion being infilled with glass and brick, with tiled panels cladding the monolithic wings. Glass blocks are also used on the staircase towers on the street side. This vocabulary, more elaborate than the plain walls of Highpoint I, was felt by many critics at the time to suggest an undue preoccupation with formal expression, despite the fact that all the materials are logically employed. In the first block the structure 'was' the architecture, or at least could be deemed to be so by those of a Functionalist mindset inclined to ignore the scrupulous artistic composition and proportion of Lubetkin's controlling hand. At Highpoint II the structure also played a decisive rôle, but one that required the complementary contributions of infilling and cladding. While Highpoint I could be apprehended as a single sculpted object, its neighbour was a visual narrative of its own process of assembly. It was not so much the materials themselves that caused concern as the overt deliberation of their use. Lubetkin was certainly more ready than his audience to move on from what he saw as the essentially diagramatic character of Highpoint I, and was quick to realize that the International Style conventions, to which it might be thought to give credence, could be taken no further. In essence he had reached the equivalent position to Le Corbusier at Villa Savoye (1930). But whereas for Le Corbusier this stylistic catharsis was to lead to a quite contrary language of formal expressionism and a monumental vernacular, as exemplified at Ronchamp and the Unité d'Habitation, Marseille, Lubetkin remained essentially committed to further exploration and enrichment of the rationalist dialect.

36. Highpoint II, 1936–38. View towards the entrance façade, a grid classically composed to contrast with the mature cedar in front.

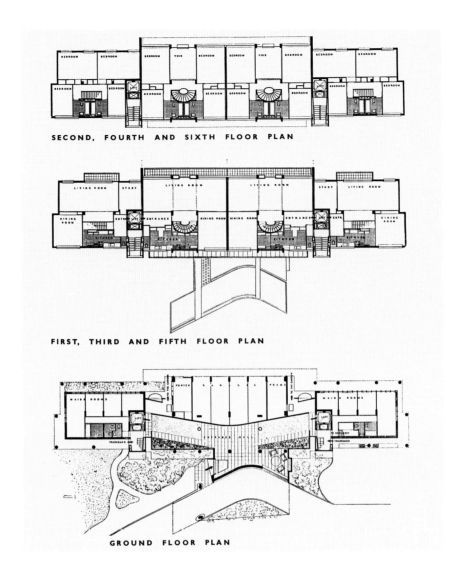

SECOND, FOURTH AND SIXTH FLOOR PLAN

FIRST, THIRD AND FIFTH FLOOR PLAN

GROUND FLOOR PLAN

38. Highpoint II plans. As at Highpoint I, the ground floor is arranged to equalize access to the two cores, while on the upper floors the staircases provide a lyrical contrast to the otherwise orthogonal geometry.

Indeed, Lubetkin had never considered modern architecture to be limited to the efficient fulfilment of its operational requirements. His artistic sensibilities ranged far beyond the narrow, or, as he would say, "mechanistic", preoccupations of Functionalism, and he felt none of the inhibition of his contemporaries in admitting the rôle of artistic will in progressive building design. So it is quite consistent with his rejection of the bleakness that he associated with orthodox Modernism that he chose the entrance porch at Highpoint II as the opportunity for a defiant demonstration of the larger, more poetic and allusive qualities that he believed must remain a vital part of contemporary architecture [39]. Nor is it surprising that his solution, using facsimile Greek caryatids, should have produced howls of protest from home-grown Modernists, who saw this as nothing less than a betrayal of the cause by its leading hero.

Though Lubetkin himself explained the use of these figures – "standardized sculptural building components" – as a means of expressing the porch as a mediation between the naturalism of the garden and the formality of the main building, as a resonant human gesture of welcome, there was also a distinct element of self-parody in his typically Tectonic comparative analysis of less suitable alternatives. This making

39. The entrance porch at Highpoint II – a poetic opus linking building and garden.

light of Modernism's own methodology evidently infuriated his contemporaries even more than did the caryatids themselves, but it is their radical structural use and their reach beyond Modernism's range of reference that now seems more enduring. Structurally, their success in diverting attention from the enormous bracket supporting the other end of the canopy only adds to the novelty of seeing these figures – invariably used symmetrically in conventional trabeation – 'job sharing' with a concrete cantilever, thereby imparting to the composition a quite unaccountable lightness. Just as at the Penguin Pool, where the massive ramp supports were disguised, here again Lubetkin and Arup's collaborative ingenuity is revealed in expressing structure where it is communicative and suppressing it elsewhere.

The breach of Modernism's conventional reference system was more subtle but no less significant. The assertion that architecture has a storyline beyond the presentation of its own technical solutions indicates Lubetkin's communion with the world of metaphor. For, unlike the nearest prior example, the 'brand-new' caryatids at St Pancras Church, London, the Highpoint figures are casts of the *damaged* figures from the Erechtheion in Athens, serving thus as symbols of time past and signifying the relativity of Modernism's preoccupation with a supposedly unending present.

40. The penthouse interior at Highpoint I, an exotic fusion of histories and cultures.

It is also necessary to remember the contemporary context to appreciate the double-edged nature of this artistic gesture. The caryatids' creativity lies in the way their novel application succeeded in offending both groups of Lubetkin's adversaries simultaneously – the Modernists obviously, but also traditionalist diehards who could apprehend classical usage only in the habitual academic way. Their appropriation by the Post-modern cause thirty years later overlooked the fact that in their own day they represented a challenge not to one but to both contending orthodoxies, the traditional and the modern.

The maverick artistic personality of Lubetkin is still more evident in the penthouse that he designed on the rooftop of Highpoint II as the main building was nearing completion [40]. This intensely personal statement, perhaps the most intimate revelation of his artistic personality in his entire œuvre, also bears out the continuing vitality of his Russian sources: the cosy fireside with its boardmarked mantel, the hand-sewn animal pelts turned to domestic advantage as in the cabin of a resourceful trapper, the roughened timber panelling recalling Russia's ancient traditions of wooden construction, the generous rough-pile rug laced in sections with coloured cords and brass rings, the home-made 'peasant' furniture – unique pieces of soft sculpture designed with his wife Margaret.

Yet it is also a world in which other elements and cultures seem to cohabit with ease. Lubetkin plays off the geometric purity of the shell ceiling against a rich collage of daily necessities and *objets trouvés*. On the travertine shelf stands a Chinese tripod pot; Pollock's Theatre prints are 'flyposted' on the kitchen wall; on other walls are hung a Dutch *trompe l'œil* triptych, marine paintings by Emile Pajot and a gouache by Fernand Léger. The entrance door is decorated with magnified images of amoebae and plankton, while from other vantage points hang mobiles specially made and installed by Lubetkin's friend Alexander Calder.

The Penthouse's interior has been variously noted for its "ephemeral décor" and "overt decorative Surrealism", which arguably provide a stylistic classification. But it may be more useful to place Lubetkin's exotic vision within another tradition of modernity, in contradistinction to the supposed mainline of Gropius, Meyer and Marinetti; a richer, more inclusive, more liberating counter-formulation represented by such artists as Stravinsky, Joyce, Picasso, Eliot and Proust that embraces metaphor, irony and multiple meaning, a tradition that accommodates humanity and its past.

All this may appear to have taken us a long way from Lubetkin's early socialist aspirations, and we now have to go back a few years to examine the fourth – and most politically focused – strand of his work in the 1930s. Soon after his arrival and introduction to the gathering circle of young Modernists, Lubetkin became involved in a number of radical groups. The first, the Modern Architectural ReSearch (or MARS) Group, was established in 1933. Though by nature a non-joiner, Lubetkin, together with a splinter group of several Tecton members, contributed significantly to a MARS exhibition project of 1934 that studied the economic, social and environmental history of the east London district of Bethnal Green. The overtly political nature of the presentation was not unanimously shared by the main group, whose preferred agenda favoured research into modern architecture's stylistic and technical aspects. Though the MARS Group went on to mount a successful exhibition on modern architecture in 1938 and to publish an alternative plan for post-war London in 1942, Lubetkin's allegiance soon transferred to the more determinedly political Architects and Technicians Organization (ATO). This was set up by Lubetkin with Francis Skinner and others to examine housing conditions generally and pursue various campaigns challenging national government policy. ATO also produced an important exhibition on contemporary housing in 1936, and was successful in mobilizing debate on housing issues and tenants' rights, supporting rent strikes against unscrupulous landlords and exposing jerry-building by speculative housing developers. But, being largely dependent on the gratuitous input of time and funds by working members, the group was relatively short-lived. Its remit passed in turn to the Association of Architects, Surveyors and Technical Assistants and thereafter to the Association of Building Technicians, both of which were largely concerned with trade-union issues, which Lubetkin also supported, albeit remaining personally unengaged.

While these extramural activities provided an outlet for Lubetkin's political energies, they produced no architecture, and the ideal of social building remained a quest that he pursued within Tecton. A high-profile competition promoted by the

41. Tecton's winning entry for the Cement Marketing Company's Competition for Working Class Flats, 1935.

1. FLEXIBILITY

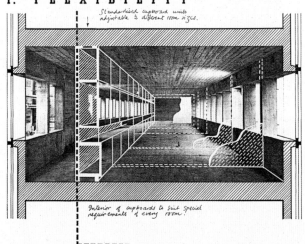

Standardised cupboard units adjustable to different room sizes.

Interior of cupboards to suit special requirements of every room.

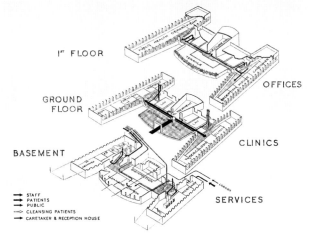

1st FLOOR

GROUND FLOOR

BASEMENT

OFFICES

CLINICS

SERVICES

→ STAFF
→ PATIENTS
→ PUBLIC
⇢ CLEANSING PATIENTS
→ CARETAKER & RECEPTION HOUSE

Cement Marketing Company in 1935 as a product-marketing exercise provided one opportunity for applying some of the lessons of Highpoint to the design of modern 'working-class' flats [41]. Tecton's winning design incorporated many features that would be developed and refined in its later work. This too, however, remained only a paper project.

It was in the work undertaken for the Metropolitan Borough of Finsbury in east central London that Lubetkin's socialist aspirations found their architectural fulfilment. Even this connection owed its origins to Godfrey Samuel inasmuch as an experimental project conducted within Tecton to compensate for early lack of work had been based on a notional brief from Samuel's family doctor. Exhibited at the British Medical Association Centenary of 1932, Tecton's clear and thoughtful design for a TB clinic on a notional site in east London made a lasting impression on a certain Dr Katial. Three years later, as Chairman of Finsbury Council's Public Health Committee, Katial invited Tecton to advise on his project for a new health centre, thus setting Lubetkin on the path towards all his public-sector work.

Finsbury was one of several 'dissident' East End councils in the 1930s whose programme would challenge national government policy. Its leaders had ambitious ideas for developing a whole plan of social building for the borough. The commissioning of Tecton in 1935, the first such recruitment of a young firm of modern architects by a client with a political constituency, was in itself a bold move on the part of Katial and his colleague, the firebrand council leader Harold Riley. While these two were certainly aware of the Highpoint I apartments completed that year and appreciated Tecton's fresh approach to planning and design through some of its other published works, the firm was hardly underwritten by the conventional credentials or public-sector track record that would nowadays be the first prerequisite for such an appointment.

The first project was to be the Health Centre in Pine Street [42], which Tecton completed in 1938. This remarkable building, which is now listed Grade I, stands as the most complete realization to be achieved during that decade of those three constituent themes of modern architecture: the reforming social agenda, the exploitation of innovative techniques and the radical modern aesthetic. Its operational aim was for a systematic and borough-wide rationalization and expansion of public-health services with the provision of a range of co-ordinated clinical facilities, and can be seen to presage by a full decade the reforms of the National Health Service.

Establishing the model of a now familiar but then unprecedented building type was but one of the project's numerous innovations. The first question confronting Tecton and its client was what identity and ambience the building should have. Lubetkin recalled early discussions with Dr Katial suggesting the atmosphere should resemble that of a club, but one that anyone should feel free to enter without the need for membership or the intimidation typically associated with hospital buildings and the medical profession – a pioneering example of what might now be called 'social inclusion'. Indeed, the initial scheme had proposed to avoid any reception desk and simply furnish the main foyer informally with coffee-tables and easy

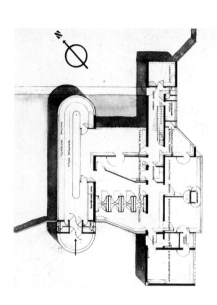

47. Tecton's unbuilt design for a TB clinic, 1932 – the progenitor of Finsbury Health Centre.

(Opposite, clockwise from top)

42. Finsbury Health Centre, London, 1935–38 – a vision of public-sector healthcare ten years before the National Health Service.

43. The foyer of Finsbury Health Centre, informally furnished with no desk, and conceived as the saloon of a club or small hotel.

44. Finsbury Health Centre's layout showing systematic organization of functions in essentially a Beaux-Arts plan

45. One of Gordon Cullen's health promotional murals in the foyer.

46. The structural solution of the clinical wings, allowing flexibility of servicing and partition layout.

48. Model of the unbuilt Busaco Street Housing Project, Finsbury, 1937–39, eventually realized as Priory Green (see fig. 58).

chairs, like the saloon lounge of a small hotel [43]. This benign scenario envisaged visitors settling themselves and being greeted by a nurse asking how she could be of assistance – a regime that would inevitably be compromised by the growing demands of administration.

The plans show Lubetkin's skill in systematic organization of a complex brief [44]. Again, his classical background is evident in the symmetrical Beaux-Arts organization, the central reception block, with its foyer, terrace and lecture theatre, leading to the two clinical wings, splayed out in what Lubetkin intended as a welcoming image of accessibility and the benefits of better health. This use of the building itself as a promotional vehicle was further developed in the foyer, where lifestyle slogans and educational murals were added by Gordon Cullen [45]. Unlike the fixed central block, the clinical wings were arranged to enable the partitions and rooms to be modified as different clinical programmes were developed [46]. The original provision included special children's and women's clinics, a dental surgery, podiatry services, a solarium, facilities for disinfection, a reception flat for displaced families and a mortuary, in addition to the lecture theatre and administrative offices. The same rational design logic of the clinical programme permeates the planning and the detail to embrace construction and servicing. The structure, which was again devised in collaboration with Arup, makes use of load-bearing mullions and deep-channel beams faced with one of the first curtain-wall systems. This left the interior partitions as non-structural elements capable of being set out from any mullion, and allowed for services within the outer ducts to be maintained and modified with minimal disruption.

Though less glamorous than Highpoint, Finsbury Health Centre is no less innovative. Its recognition of services and adaptability as fundamental determinants of progressive building design superseded the contemporary preoccupation with

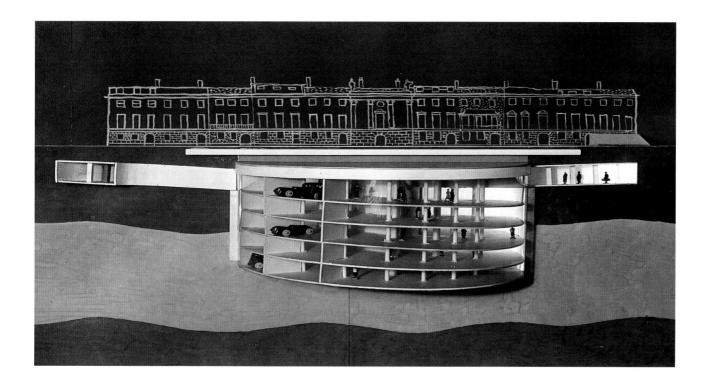

49. Cutaway model of Tecton's air-raid shelter design, showing the protective thick top slab and spiral ramped accommodation, designed to convert to car-parking use in peacetime.

merely an image of Modernism, while its inclusive ambience and secular formality provided the first exemplar of a modern civic building for the Welfare State. Opened in 1938 by Lord Horder, the King's Physician, the health centre received massive press coverage and has remained in beneficial use ever since.

At the time, however, the centre was only the first element of what was intended to be a much larger programme of social building and regeneration in Finsbury. Even before its completion two large housing schemes were being commissioned from Tecton, the Busaco Street and Sadler Street projects, both of which were to be halted by the War. The first of these [48], however, was developed to an advanced stage, and was certainly significant in securing Lubetkin's subsequent re-engagement.

In the closing years of the 1930s Tecton's work for Finsbury was perforce redirected to the planning of air-raid precautions, an issue given sudden and alarming urgency by the Munich crisis of 1938. This proved a controversial and, for Lubetkin, frustrating assignment. Following typically thorough Tecton research, which included Francis Skinner travelling to Spain to study the effects of aerial bombing in the Civil War, a scheme of deep concrete shelters was devised to protect the borough's entire population [49]. However, these proposals, with their considerable investment implications, conflicted with national government policy, which favoured an assortment of ARP measures, including sandbagged cellars, propped basements and the notorious and flimsy Anderson shelters, lightweight corrugated-metal shells for individual householders to install in their own gardens.

Tecton's scheme for Finsbury, published in the monograph *Planned ARP* (1939) and determinedly backed by the council's leaders, represented a direct challenge to the Home Office and was refused subsidy. Churchill himself denounced the proposals, describing the practice's assessment of the dangers of air attack as exaggerated and

50. Berthold and Margaret Lubetkin (née Church) photographed at The Stork Club, New York, in 1937 during the Museum of Modern Art's exhibition *Modern Architecture in England.*

51. Upper Kilcott Farm, near Chipping Sodbury, Gloucestershire, Lubetkin's home from 1940 to 1962.

the wider circulation of the book as "unhelpful at the present juncture". Finsbury's attempts to initiate the first shelter at Busaco Street were legally blocked, and, as Tecton disbanded at the outbreak of war, Lubetkin ended this period of extraordinary productivity and acclaim by receiving his first taste of official rejection.

In the space of less than ten years he had established himself and Tecton as the foremost practitioners of modern architecture in England, with a series of works whose aesthetic and technical brilliance would come to epitomize the architectural aspirations of the era. Though the largest commissions of his professional career were still all ahead of him, the post-war world was to prove a less congenial environment for his idiosyncratic creativity. The next generation of modern architects would appear on the scene and a new and larger chapter in modern architecture's development was to displace Lubetkin's unique early pre-eminence.

In 1939 Lubetkin was naturalized as a British citizen and married Margaret Church (1917–1978), a talented architect in her own right [50], who had joined Tecton from the Architectural Association as a young assistant in the mid-1930s. Their departure to Gloucestershire the following year to take up farming is often and incorrectly interpreted as a premature retirement, though being rendered professionally inactive by the War and being ineligible for call-up would, for Lubetkin,

52. The Lenin Memorial, Holford Square, London, 1942, designed by Lubetkin for Finsbury Council. (Lenin's bust was provided by the Soviet Embassy in London.)

have made a move of some sort unavoidable. It is nonetheless understandable how his suddenly leaving the limelight of London and the sophistication of the Highpoint penthouse for the rustic depths of Chipping Sodbury [51] has been conflated with his later withdrawal from professional prominence in the 1950s.

However, to attribute to Lubetkin at this stage in his career a determination to quit architecture altogether would be to misconstrue his position. Though he was disappointed at the loss of his more radical earlier expectations, this relocation was essentially his and Margaret's personal response to the vast change of circumstances that would affect the lives of all sections of society in different ways. Indeed, at the same moment as retreating to the country, he applied for registration under the Architects' Registration Act (1931), and in any case continued to use the penthouse on his visits to London both during the War and for a period afterwards.

Even Lubetkin's connection with Finsbury was not interrupted for long. In 1941, in the wave of pro-Soviet solidarity that followed Russia's decision to join the Allies, he was invited to design a Lenin Memorial [52] in Holford Square (where the great Marxist leader had briefly stayed at an early period of his life), and as early as 1943 he was commissioned to resume work on the Sadler Street housing project, which started on site in 1946 and was completed in 1950 as the Spa Green Estate.

The new economic, political and social context in which this next chapter of Lubetkin's work occurred should not obscure the fact that it grew organically out of his pre-war experience. Nor should the acknowledgement that it might not possess quite the glamour and acclaim of, say, Highpoint or the Penguin Pool detract from its enormous accomplishment and creative energy. Lubetkin's post-war work, just like that of Le Corbusier, needs to be read as a critical commentary on contemporaneous architectural activity and shows how architects of this calibre adapted and extended their technical and artistic range to the more complex challenge of the new situation. In Lubetkin's case a number of clear preoccupations may be identified, notably the search for a new urban order, continuing technical advancement and the further evolution of structural typologies, and – most controversially – the related development of an expressive architectural vocabulary to suit the larger scale of building development.

All these themes are exhibited at Spa Green [53], which fairly bristles with innovation, and which, being now listed, stands as arguably the most accomplished metropolitan social-housing scheme of Britain's first phase of post-war reconstruction. Its layout embodies a strategic placing of high and low blocks, in the latter case subtly inflected towards the adjoining nineteenth-century terraced housing, and the creation of a 'reservoir' of urban space defined by the buildings but opening to a larger area of landscaping and civic gardens [54]. In generic terms the thesis is clearly Corbusian, an endorsement of the principles of space, sunlight and verdure that were intended to supersede the congestion and monotony of the nineteenth-century corridor street. Yet the characterful identity of the blocks themselves, their human touches and their acutely sensitive fit to site make the scheme anything but anonymous.

The structural solution, in which Ove Arup again collaborated, is of particular interest. Here, completing the inversion of the 'eggshell' system of Highpoint I, is a box-frame or 'eggcrate' structure [55], which Arup had been developing through the war years for bombproof buildings. The structural walls are arranged transversely to the main axis of the building, thus leaving the elevations open to a variety of alternative treatments. This liberating opportunity Lubetkin was to seize with all the architectural imagination at his command. In his allusive mind these cross-wall structures and floor strata were a precise equivalent of the warp and weft of the traditional carpet, a matrix for communicative infilling. Just as the repetitive rhythms of those carpets he had studied on his travels had revealed their visual metaphors and encrypted meanings, so for Lubetkin these large, contemporary façades could become an abstract narrative through the organization of their constituent elements into a whole composition [56, 57].

This highly inventive formal enrichment was to become a characteristic of the firm's ensuing work and was explored in a prolific range of applications to suit the circumstances of the scheme in hand. It may be seen as a logical extension of the considered composition of Highpoint II's cladding, and duly prompted further misgivings from orthodox critics who regarded this as no more than gratuitous

(Opposite, clockwise from top left)

53. Spa Green, 1943–50, technically innovative and architecturally assured, setting the standard for early post-war social housing.

54. Spa Green site plan, an urban composition of two eight-storey blocks and a serpentine lower block, a 'spatial reservoir' with estate landscaping and civic gardens.

55. Spa Green box-frame structure in course of construction.

56. Spa Green lower-block façade, a three-dimensional chequered composition set in a cream-tiled frame.

57. Caucasian kilim referred to by Lubetkin in explaining his façade designs.

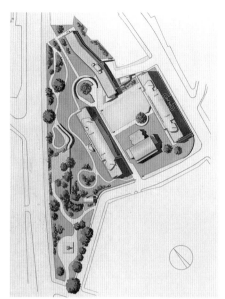

58. Model of the Priory Green Estate, 1943–57 (altered in execution), showing the large central square.

59. Aerial view of Bevin Court, 1946–54, showing the large Y-shaped block and the nearer smaller block (Holford House) in their geometric urban setting.

60. The Hallfield Estate, Paddington, 1946–54: large-scale urban housing with mature landscaped courts of commensurate size.

'pattern-making'. But while the resulting designs may certainly be enjoyed as patterns, it is really as a challenge to the bleakness and mechanical repetition so characteristic of modern mass housing that Lubetkin's efforts are properly understood. Regardless of whether the average passer-by observing the façades of Spa Green, or its sequels, may apprehend that he is seeing the built echoes of a Caucasian kilim, the continuing care and vigour in this area of Lubetkin's work, not to mention its unusual popularity, make a compelling case in view of the subsequent castigation of modern architecture for its relentless poverty of expression. His compositions were intended as urban tapestries, weaving the elements of mass housing into a total dynamic design. To Lubetkin, this was not "mere formalism"; it was a matter of formality, responding to larger civic obligations, beyond the detailed domestic circumstances of the flats themselves. The effect on the blocks' perceived scale and sense of resolution is decisive, as is the careful tiled edging treatment, functioning like a carpet's borders, that finishes the presentation with such clarity and definition.

The same themes are explored with equal inventiveness in the next schemes for Finsbury: Priory Green, an enlarged redevelopment of the pre-war Busaco Street project; and Holford Square, a wholly post-war commission arising from bomb damage during the Blitz. Though having a less favourable site context and suffering unfortunate budget cuts during design development, Priory Green (now a Conservation Area) is nevertheless set out on a generous scale in the first attempt to reinterpret the traditional London square in a modern idiom [58]. The blocks themselves, using cross-wall construction, like Spa Green, are also characterized by vigorous rhythmic façade chequering that serves to bind the separate buildings into a dramatic ensemble. Meanwhile, Holford Square, being too expensive to reconstruct in a similar form, was reconfigured in the triaxial block Bevin Court in a dynamic response to the geometry of the surrounding neighbourhood [59]. Also now listed, it contains a central staircase [61] that brings the energy of these urban environs into the heart of the building. This element alone is as powerful an architectonic statement as anything in the whole Lubetkin canon and stands as a masterpiece of sculptural form and spatial imagination.

The last in this series of early post-war housing projects was the Hallfield Estate in Paddington, west London [60], which, along with Churchill Gardens in Pimlico, was probably one of the largest central urban housing redevelopments in England at the time. Unlike that scheme, however, in which blocks of various sizes and bland appearance are distributed in a pragmatic and uncomposed manner, Hallfield is planned formally on a bold, diagonal grid of two contrasting and characterful block types to produce a series of interlocking 'urban rooms' of splendid scale and landscape quality. It is this distinctive preoccupation with planning and urban form that was now to open a new and crucial chapter in Lubetkin's career.

In 1947 Lubetkin was offered the appointment as Architect Planner of Peterlee New Town in County Durham, in the north-east of England. With the struggle of realizing the London housing projects already becoming wearisome, this opportunity suddenly promised a challenge of a quite different order. His initial

61. The radial staircase at Bevin Court, a listed sculptural masterpiece.

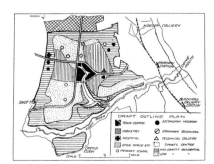

62. Lubetkin's unrealized draft masterplan, 1950. The town centre (shaded) is shown around the top of the upper gorge, Blunts Dene

scepticism having been overcome by categorical undertakings of official support, Lubetkin accepted the post to wide acclaim and embarked on the project with recharged expectations. Though Tecton's long-term future was already in some doubt, this assignment now made its dissolution inevitable. Thus none of the foregoing projects was completed in the lifetime of the partnership, which was formally dissolved in 1948, the Finsbury work being taken forward by Francis Skinner with Lubetkin's assistance when available, and Hallfield being developed and executed by Lindsay Drake and Denys Lasdun in a newly formed practice.

Peterlee was the seventh new town to be designated under the 1946 New Towns Act. The key attraction for Lubetkin was that it would be a town for miners, a fiercely cohesive occupational group, and that it was an exercise in concentration rather than dispersal, bringing together the existing populations of the surrounding villages into a compact urban nucleus. Indeed the idea for a new centre to supersede the squalor and deprivation of the area's industrial past had originated within the local community itself. Another decisive factor was that the town should be built fast, partly to reinforce its centripetal 'pull', partly to minimize the adverse consequences of suspending investment in the existing villages. Thus, despite post-war scarcities, Peterlee was to be accorded top priority in the provision of labour and material resources.

Added to these compelling political and social aims was an inspirational site – a wide, gently concave bowl of virgin land, split by spectacular gorges. Two of these, Castle Eden Dene, which led right out to the North Sea, and Blunts Dene, a tributary of the larger Castle Eden Dene, would frame and penetrate the main development. This topography meant that the whole town could be contained within the horizon line of the Designated Area, eliminating the sight, the noise and the associations of the pithead gear and spoil heaps around the outside.

Such preconditions seemed to promise Lubetkin everything he had dreamed of, and his appointment and reputation raised expectations of an outstanding outcome. "The greatest opportunity in town planning for centuries" and "the greatest building adventure since the construction of Bath" were typical headlines in the euphoric contemporary press coverage.

But the project was fatally flawed. While it had been assumed by all concerned that the town's main industry would continue to be mining, astonishingly no prior consideration had been given to the implications of building over the active coalfield and the onerous difficulties of subsidence and compensation. The Designated Area overlay valuable seams of unmined coal that were expected to secure the area's economic future for decades. To avoid the problem, only the lightest and dispersed form of building could be considered, and any high building must await completion of the underlying coal extraction and subsequent settlement. Such assumptions had indeed been established between the two departments concerned – the Ministry of Town and Country Planning and the National Coal Board – in discussions that preceded Lubetkin's appointment. Within weeks of his arrival on the scene he began to see his vision for a dense, coherent city being downgraded to a formless sprawl of suburban villas that might take decades to achieve.

Lubetkin immediately urged wholesale reconsideration of this prior concordat, advancing various technical and administrative strategies for co-ordinating overground and underground operations that would allow the planning of a compact town. But the degree of official motivation and co-operation that such an approach required was not forthcoming, and over the next two years the project became paralysed by vexatious disputes between the government departments and within the Development Corporation. Indeed, on two occasions the problems of Peterlee were referred to the Cabinet for resolution. In 1950, however, after two years of frustration and with not a single house built, Lubetkin left Peterlee in despair.

Nonetheless, a few surviving plans give some indication of Lubetkin's vision [62, 63]. Served from the A19 trunk road, which he had wanted to reorientate towards the town via a spectacular bridge, the town centre is located at the end of Blunts Dene, with further bridges and causeways linking the different parts. Lubetkin's design explodes the triaxial motif of Bevin Court to produce a central reservoir of space, poised on the fingertips of three substantial residential blocks, primary urban markers, whose axes intersect in mid-air across the Dene and whose splayed sides in

63. One of several detailed studies of Lubetkin's proposed town-centre design. Three large residential blocks serve as urban markers to define the urban centre functions grouped around Blunts Dene.

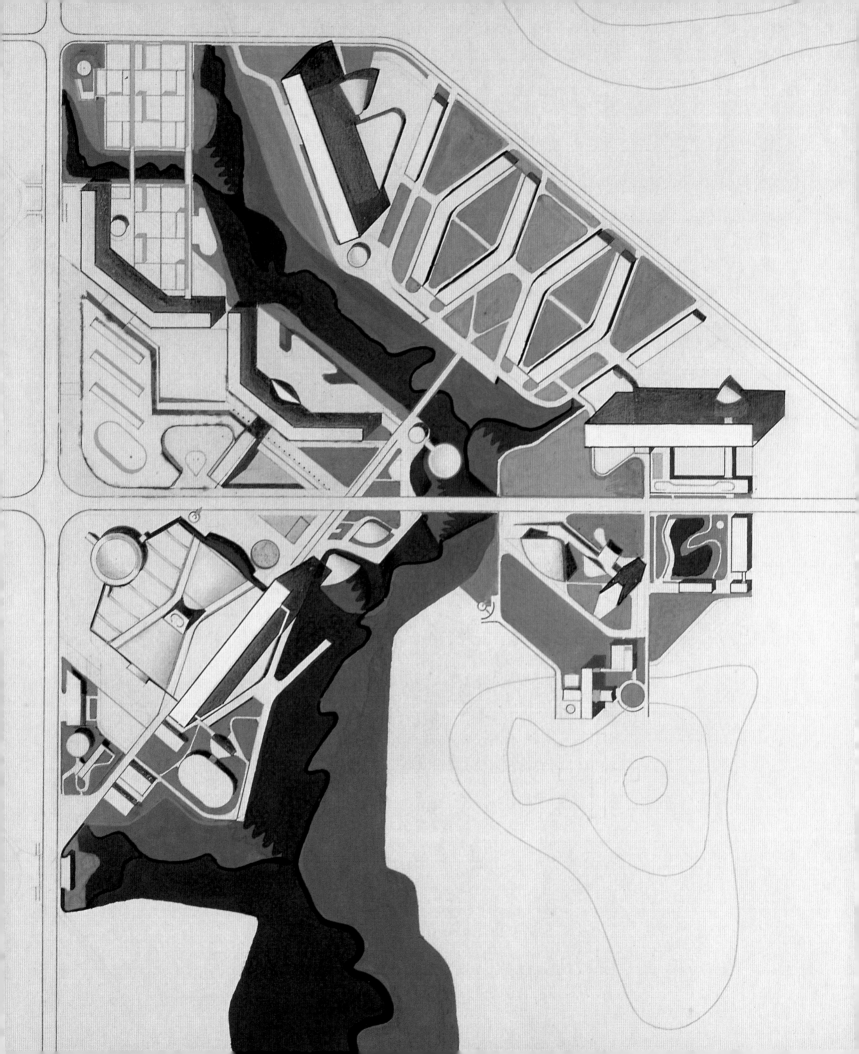

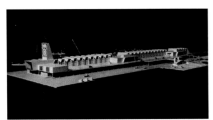

64. Study model of terraced miners' housing developed by Lubetkin's Peterlee team, 1949.

65. Lubetkin on the farm in Gloucestershire in the 1950s.

66. Unbuilt project for Ocean Terminal Building, Karachi, by Skinner, Bailey & Lubetkin, c. 1952–55.

67. Spiral staircase at Sivil House, Bethnal Green, designed by Lubetkin.

turn define three vistas opening to the infinity of the horizon. Into and around this vortex were to be placed the various functions of the town centre – the transport terminal, the civic centre, and retail, leisure and cultural buildings – geometrical abstractions against the untamed landscape of the wooded gorge.

These drawings should not be misconstrued. As finite artwork compositions they might suggest an unrealistic formal determinacy, whereas they are really shorthand for a larger proposition: the idea of an energized spatial matrix, defined, as Lubetkin himself was later to relate, "by architectural strong points, kind of Martello towers … and by strengthening these so much that subsequent development of their surroundings, although spread over a period of years, would be powerless to spoil the main vision of the town". Another illustration [64] shows some of the preliminary designs that Lubetkin and his team developed for the miners' houses that would be distributed in terraces around the town centre. Their aim, as he put it, was "to paraphrase in terms of continuity of form, the solidarity of the mining community itself".

However, none of these creative proposals was to be adopted and with Lubetkin's departure the new town project was developed by others working to a wholly different philosophy. Lubetkin's Peterlee entered the folklore of British Modernism as one of its tragic lost causes and the greatest opportunity of his career turned out to be its greatest disappointment. He returned to the farm in Gloucestershire [65], profoundly and permanently wounded, his retreat from Peterlee becoming synonymous with his retirement from professional practice altogether.

The ensuing reality, however, was less conclusive. For although Lubetkin did indeed withdraw from public prominence, he continued to remain involved in architecture over the next fifteen years through the re-formed practice of himself, Francis Skinner, one of his original Tecton partners, and Douglas Bailey, his deputy from Peterlee. An initial period of reorientation in the early 1950s saw a variety of prospects come and go: a large conference hotel complex in New Delhi, India; possible appointment to the new capital city of Chandigarh, a commission that later passed to Le Corbusier; and a major ocean terminal for the port of Karachi [66]. The firm also entered several architectural competitions, but without success.

Soon, however, Lubetkin and his younger colleagues re-established a steady source of work through their engagement with the Metropolitan Borough of Bethnal Green, which, like Finsbury, was another east London borough suffering historic problems of economic and social deprivation. Here a new series of housing projects was undertaken, with Lubetkin contributing to the key planning decisions and architectural elements. As with Bevin Court, the staircases in some of these schemes are particularly fine and exemplify Lubetkin's sculptural talent at its most vigorous [67]. The studied architectural characterization also continues and develops the distinctive 'chequered carpet' themes from Finsbury [68].

Lubetkin's central preoccupation in these final works is, however, the application of the urban design ideals thwarted at Peterlee, specifically the concept of, as he termed it, "the spatial vector" – the urban ensemble unified not by its architecture

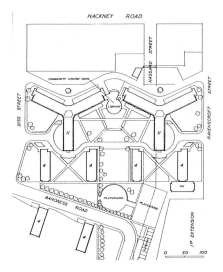

68. Detail of Sivill House façade, where the alternate configuration of windows and cladding panels is derived from the stylized dragon motif of traditional Caucasian carpets.

69. Dorset Estate, 1951–57: site plan showing formal composition of elements.

70. Lakeview Estate, 1953–56, with diametrical interrelationship of blocks.

as such but by space "energized" by its architectural co-ordinates. This powerful idea, in contradistinction to what he saw as Le Corbusier's increasing and misguided preoccupation with large, 'stand-alone' blocks, or '*unités*', was absorbed even from his earliest experiences of St Petersburg and Paris, and was now to dominate his approach. Even contemporary developments in the Soviet Union, which he revisited in 1953 after Stalin's death, became a source of comparative inspiration – not of course for their faux-classical architectural style but for their grand spatial organization and sense of coherence.

Several familiar themes coalesce – the unifying rôle of the axis, hitherto largely deployed within the single building; the preoccupation with movement, the *promenade architecturale*, now enlarged to an urban scale; the contrived contrast of formal and informal landscape; the 'talking façade', now in group conversation – all to fuse in Lubetkin's interpretation of that key formative idea, the spatial vector, an implied forcefield binding together land, buildings and urban space in a total composition – a modern *Gesamtkunstwerk*.

Here, as elsewhere in Lubetkin's œuvre, there are aspects of his position that may be identified with the mainstream Modern Movement: the raised block, the mix of heights, the expansive landscapes to be appreciated as much as abstract compositions when viewed from above as amenities experienced at ground level. But there are also others that mark his distinctive and perhaps unique contribution: answers to the new problems of land design, civic ensemble and customization to local context.

From the early post-war years the oncoming generation of architects was beginning to challenge the orthodox Modernist town-planning system embodied in Le Corbusier's treatise *La Ville Radieuse* (1935). But whereas this increasing dissatisfaction led many of these 'third-generation' Modernists to explore various topological approaches, urban megastructures and notably the idea of 'the street in the sky' (as realized most fully in the massive Park Hill development in Sheffield), Lubetkin continued to pursue what was essentially his own agenda, infusing the original generic elements of modern planning with his distinctive architectural characterization and unifying his compositions with that formative concept – the spatial vector. Indeed, it might be said that while others sought to reinvent traditional solutions in novel building forms, Lubetkin, using established forms of modern building, went back into urban history in search of new answers to the vital question of their interrelationship.

The first two projects for Bethnal Green, the Dorset and Lakeview Estates [69, 70], were limited by briefing and site constraints. It was the last and the largest of these late housing commissions in east London, at Cranbrook, just south-west of Victoria Park, that allowed his most ambitious demonstration of these ideas. Exploiting the unusual oblique street patterns of the neighbourhood, Lubetkin organizes the vast 7-hectare (17-acre) site on the intersection of two diagonal axes. Around these is disposed a group of six towers ranging from eleven to fifteen storeys and diametrically paired off by height and orientation to produce a rotating

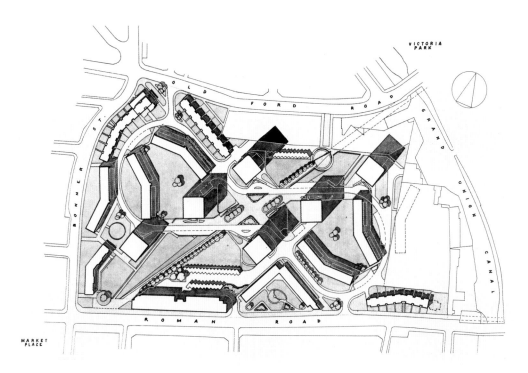

71. (Left) Cranbrook Estate site plan, showing the six towers paired by height and orientation, with other blocks diminishing towards the periphery. The intended park connection and *trompe l'œil* sculpture are shown, upper right.

72. (Below) Aerial view of Cranbrook Estate, by Skinner, Bailey & Lubetkin, 1955–65, with Victoria Park top right.

73. Cranbrook Estate *trompe l'œil*, 1965, preserving an illusion of the journey beyond.

'centrifuge' [71]. The energy at the core radiates outwards in a fanning series of maisonette blocks, which, together with the still smaller terraces and houses, reconcile the estate's perimeter with the scale of its Victorian surroundings.

Architecture parlante, buildings in dialogue across space, the concept of 'becoming' imparted by spiral diametry, horizontal and vertical progression – the entire range of Lubetkin's creative arsenal is deployed in the drive for urban coherence, the spatial vector of the central avenue providing the vital armature [72].

But this declamatory masterwork of three-dimensional planning, replete with Lubetkin's lessons from St Petersburg and Paris, was not quite the conclusion. The council's failure to make available the last fragment of land that would have permitted the avenue to reach the park provoked a final addendum. Lubetkin's *trompe l'œil* sculpture [73], installed at the site's north-east corner to suggest the imagined journey beyond, perhaps surpasses even the Highpoint caryatids as an attempt at transforming historical reference into current usage. An act of inventiveness and imagination of which surely no other contemporary would have been capable, it underlines his marginalization in public and professional comprehension at the end of his active career and, indeed, defies all the conventional architectural classifications of its period.

Completed in 1966, Cranbrook was Lubetkin's last public artistic statement, after which he did effectively retire from professional practice but for a few minor private commissions. In the later 1950s he had contemplated emigration to China, but in the event relinquished the farm in 1962, finally moving to Bristol in 1969.

For the next dozen years he lived in almost complete obscurity, reinforced by a period of profound mourning following Margaret Lubetkin's death in 1978. Thus his story might easily have ended. Yet, extraordinarily, there was still a final chapter to follow. In 1982, after discreet but dedicated campaigning by a few devotees, Lubetkin was rediscovered and awarded the Royal Gold Medal by the Royal Institute of British Architects [74], and for the last years of his life enjoyed a new phase of international acclaim sustained by lecturing and travels.

When Lubetkin died in 1990 the British Modern Movement lost its first original hero. Yet while he was unquestionably a part and a product of the Modern Movement, he was also one of its most intelligent critics. He was once characterized as "a man of eighteenth-century charm, nineteenth-century thrust, preoccupied with twenty-first-century problems", a description that suggests both the time frame within which he might be considered and also, as it were by default, the fascinating difficulty of placing him in his own century – the twentieth. The trajectory of his career – from the optimism and brilliance of the 1930s to the vexed struggles of the post-war period, and the debacle of Peterlee – might be seen as a paradigm of modern architecture as a whole and its declining social consensus. Yet it is unfair, as well as uninformative, to discount Lubetkin's later, more difficult but less glamorous work simply because it complicates the popular myth of his premature retirement. It is the totality of his story that reveals the evolution and tenacity of his contribution. His better-known legacy has come to define the early Modern Movement in England, yet as a radical European intellectual he presents an incongruous figure in twentieth-century British culture, with its distinctive parochialism and incorrigible ambivalence towards modernity. The leading light who remained an outsider, it is perhaps this unique combination of the exemplary and the exotic that gives his story such durability and fascination. A rationalist with a poet's heart, he indeed achieved his aim of giving "a face to his age", but this vision extended far beyond Modernism's immediate programme and preoccupations. In judging his significance we must look beyond the conventional categories and appreciate the extraordinary range of his creativity and imagination. He sought to place modern architecture on the same level as the great architectural traditions of previous ages and pursued this aspiration with all the intellectual, technical and artistic resources at his command. Yet his understanding of how modern architecture must be informed by history never weakened his belief in its duty to set forth the vision of a better future. An extract from his Royal Gold Medal address provides both a conclusion and a challenge:

"We have to choose which tradition to follow since they now exist in parallel. Back to romantic melodrama, mortgaged, all electric manor houses with phoney chimney stacks, and the pre-slump, semi-Tudor villas screened by pretensions, or the sober eloquence of regularity with its sharp-edged spare and lucid geometry. Architectural design can be either a metaphor of the world to come or an epitaph of the one that has gone, never to come back again."

74. Berthold Lubetkin awarded the Royal Gold Medal at the Royal Institute of British Architects, 29 June 1982.

The survey that follows is both a celebration and an audit. Its object was to revisit, review and record all Lubetkin's extant buildings in 2001, the centenary of his birth (on 14 December 1901). The findings, for the most part, testify to the durability of his legacy and confirm the importance of his contribution to the Modern Movement. As Morley von Sternberg's photography shows, the outstanding architectural qualities that first projected Lubetkin and his partners on to the international stage continue to resonate. That surely is cause for celebration.

What of the audit? Buildings, like people, develop their own life stories. Their fortunes depend on a variety of factors: part nature – in the case of buildings, their original client, purpose, quality of design and construction; and part nurture – their stewardship, the correspondence between original intention and evolving function, their popularity, embodied value and sustainability.

The illustrations also show that the fortunes of Lubetkin's buildings have varied. His pre-war work is more than sixty years old and in most cases has survived a world war and over half a century of use remarkably intact. Even his post-war work is between thirty-five and fifty years old and largely continues to provide good accommodation to many hundreds of people. Some works have been conscientiously cared for, or sympathetically adapted in response to changing need. Some have been greatly changed and can now hardly be regarded as the building he, or his partnership, designed. A few have been lost altogether.

The passage of time has also altered the context in which they are seen. Modern Movement architecture is now 'heritage' and a new conservation culture has emerged to address the issue of Modern Movement icons in distress. The fact that most of Lubetkin's surviving buildings have been statutorily listed provides some reassurance that his considerable legacy will not now be damaged or demolished by default. This, however, does not necessarily prevent casual and incremental disfigurement, which can steadily erode the integrity of a fine work. Nor does it prevent simple neglect.

We hope, therefore, that this survey not only brings pleasure to admirers of this great architect, but that it also calls attention to the need for ongoing vigilance and support.

John Allan, 14 December 2001

LUBETKIN TODAY An Illustrated Survey of Works

HOUSES

Genesta Road
Heath Drive
The Beach House
Hillfield
Holly Frindle
Six Pillars
Egypt End
West Grove
Sunnywood Drive
The Wilderness

ZOO BUILDINGS

London Zoo
Gorilla House
North Gate Kiosk
Penguin Pool
Whipsnade Park
Elephant House
The Restaurant
Dudley Zoo
Entrance Building
Kiosk 1
Kiosk 2
Moat Café
Castle Restaurant
Polar Bear Pit
Bear Ravine
Aviary
Elephant House
Station Café*
Reptiliary*
Sea Lion Pool*

APARTMENTS

Avenue de Versailles
Highpoint I
Highpoint II

PUBLIC WORKS

Finsbury Council
Finsbury Health Centre
Spa Green
Priory Green
Priory Green Extension (now Priory Heights)
Bevin Court
Paddington Council
Hallfield
Bethnal Green Council
Dorset Estate
Sivill House
Lakeview
Cranbrook

LAST WORKS

Butterick Factory
Tabard Garden Estate
Club 85
St Andrew's Ambulance Association

STAIRCASES

A compilation

*Not illustrated

Nos. 85, 87, 89, 91 Genesta Road
Greenwich
London SE18

1933–34
Listed Grade II

Lubetkin & A.V. Pilichowski

Though it was Pilichowski's introduction
that secured the job, the design of this
speculative scheme of four three-storey
houses was Lubetkin's alone. Simple, stylish
and enduringly popular, their frontage
makes just sufficient acknowledgement of
the Victorian neighbours while remaining
uncompromisingly modern **(opposite)**.
After nearly seventy years the design caters
for contemporary domestic living just as
well as when the houses were built. It is
a depressing reflection that this terrace
intervention, despite adopting the most
traditional urban form in England, would
be rejected by most planning authorities
in London if proposed today.

Planar façades, cyma balcony fronts,
fenêtres en longueur **(left)** – here is
Lubetkin working out his vocabulary in
preparation for Highpoint, then on
Tecton's drawing boards.

Though the originally open rear loggia
has been enclosed to provide a ground-
floor room, Lubetkin's boldly scalloped
stair spine wall retains the sense of an
open outlook to the garden **(top)**.

The master of modern staircase design
opens his English account with this
sculptural example toplit from the
rooflight above **(above)**. The scalloped
spine at the first-floor landing creates a
sense of spaciousness despite the modest
dimensions available.

**64 Heath Drive
Gidea Park
Essex**

1933–34
Listed Grade II

Skinner & Tecton

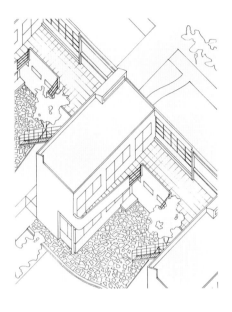

The main modifications to this prize-winning house – enclosure of the first-floor terrace and removal of the solid guarding – have not detracted from its clarity and freshness. Well cared for and recently embellished by a bespoke garden design, it stands as a solitary beacon of modernity amid the suburbia of Gidea Park.

The Beach House
Bay Walk
Aldwick Bay
West Sussex

1933–34

Chitty & Tecton

Administered by Chitty, but designed by
Lubetkin, this once elegant seaside house
was too limpidly sculptural for its aesthetic
integrity to survive the alterations and infills
of a later era. When a composition is made
of so few perfectly judged lines it takes very
little to spoil it (compare with fig. 26, p. 23).

Hillfield ('Bungalow A')
Dunstable Road
Whipsnade, near Dagnall
Buckinghamshire

1933–36
Listed Grade II*

Lubetkin & Tecton

First listed in 1988 – relatively late by comparison with Lubetkin's premier 1930s works – Hillfield at Whipsnade **(right)** and its smaller sibling, Holly Frindle, have survived a period of uncertainty but are now in safe hands. The sense of seclusion, somehow intensified by the periodic sight of a glider floating silently overhead – the beacon range being an ideal location for thermal currents – is also reinforced by encroaching vegetation (compare the view of its setting in fig. 27, p. 23). Continuous conservative repair and minimal intervention is the key to the future here, which is exactly what this jewel is receiving, thanks to the understanding of its current owner.

(Below from left) The almost impossibly slender transoms of Lubetkin's concrete screen at Hillfield are still intact, albeit visibly deflecting. But, in addition to gravity, the gentle but relentless pressure of vegetation and lichen means that his image of man's benign dominion over nature is tenable only by constant cleaning and redecoration.

The Thermolux glazed panels of Hillfield had been replaced with plywood by a previous owner, and subsequently with mica boards, but may now be reinstated. Thermolux has also disappeared from the top and bottom tiers of the projecting screen.

Hillfield's veranda, with its cantilevered sill line, still hovers immaculately over the ground, as Lubetkin intended.

A view down the loggia with its replacement spars and glass lens screen. Lubetkin's subtle sequence of semi-outdoor spaces around Hillfield remains one of its unique delights.

Holly Frindle ('Bungalow B')
Whipsnade Park
Dunstable
Bedfordshire

1933–36
Listed Grade II

Lubetkin & Tecton

Now operated as a weekend retreat for the staff of Richard Rogers Partnership, the second of Lubetkin's two bungalows at Whipsnade, only metres from the first but in a different county, has been repaired and refitted, and is in better shape than it has been for decades. The walls and panels gleam and the shadow gap separating building from ground is once again as crisp as on day one.

**Six Pillars
Crescentwood Road
Dulwich
London SE26**

**1934–35
Listed Grade II**

Harding & Tecton

This generous and elegant house has always seemed at home in the opulent south London suburb of Dulwich, and, after recent refurbishment by architect John Winter, is in good shape for an extended future. The original use of stock brick in the ground and upper floors **(right)**, as a concession to the trustees of the Dulwich Estate, gives the house a sort of dual identity that, together with the newly coloured columns, might now even be read as Post-modern.

The dancing stair **(far left)**, another leitmotif of the Tecton canon, is the spatial armature that binds the building together. This half spiral, a simple solution by Lubetkin's later standards, still imparts a sense of ceremony to the act of changing floors.

Though the cherry tree that originally 'decorated' the private façade has gone, the tightly enclosed garden **(above left)** remains a rich, secluded space. The asymmetry of the top floor above such a carefully balanced elevation still seems wilfully bizarre.

The square lattice screen **(below left)**, a Tecton trademark, was such an intelligent device for the treatment of large domestic openings – more appropriate in scale than a window, more practical than huge pieces of glass – that it is surprising it has not been more widely used since. Whether the screen is clear glazed, as here, or diffused, as at Highpoint, the fluctuating shadow pattern provides an almost hypnotic commentary on external light.

**Egypt End
(now Gordonbush House)
Egypt Lane
Burnham Beeches
Farnham Common
Buckinghamshire**

1934–35

Harding & Tecton

Only a Tecton devotee would recognize
this original work of Val Harding, so
altered is it now with enclosures and
extensions. Even the idyllic sylvan setting
has been tamed into a conventional
suburban garden. Egypt End (later renamed
Gordonbush House) has evidently responded
to changing demands but also makes the
case for documenting authentic works
before they lose their identity.

West Grove
Hammers Lane
Mill Hill
London NW7

1936–37
Listed Grade II

Tecton

The conversion of this fine Georgian house was undertaken for the owner of the house adjacent to Highpoint I, when the time came to sell up for the development of Highpoint II. Tecton's intelligent interventions, including rationalization of the planning, the addition of flint 'bookends' and the long, laterally acting first-floor beam (structurally engineered by Ove Arup) were so well integrated as to seem almost invisible **(below)**, but the gross thickening of the original spindling columns **(left)** by a subsequent owner greatly reduces the delicacy of the loggia.

Nos. 59, 61, 63, 65, 66, 68, 70, 72 Sunnywood Drive
Haywards Heath
West Sussex

1934–36

Lubetkin & Tecton

Yesterday's controversy is today's consensus. Tecton's struggle to build this group of eight speculative houses in the teeth of local opposition is forgotten history long since overlaid by the commonplace accretions of suburbia. And, as if to underline the irony, one house is now rendered white (contrary to original planning stipulations), while another has a pitched roof (contrary to the architects' predilections).

The Wilderness
Holmbury St Mary
Surrey

1938–39

Tecton

As little known in the Tecton canon as its name might suggest, this substantial house, undertaken on the very eve of the Second World War for Lord Wilfred Greene (Margaret Church's godfather), also marks the beginning of Lubetkin's 'wilderness years' of professional inactivity pending the new demands of national reconstruction.

Pitched-roofed at the insistence of the client, and with powerfully expressed balcony and parapet lines, the original house had such a strong character that subsequent alterations have made little impression on its overall identity. Well cared for and beautifully landscaped, The Wilderness remains a historical secret in the depths of Surrey.

London Zoo
Regent's Park
London NW1

Gorilla House

1932–33
Listed Grade I

Tecton

Lubetkin's first building in England, the Gorilla House at London Zoo, retains its strange allure, despite innumerable changes of occupant and fit-out, and a steady loss of authentic features – most notably the sliding screens and revolving roof, originally provided for seasonal enclosure of the climate-sensitive gorillas. Only the spokes of the roof plate remain, parked externally, giving a misleading impression of structural complexity. A temporary installation maintains the building in beneficial use pending funds for an exhibit of Madagascan lemurs.

North Gate Kiosk

1936–37
Listed Grade II

Tecton

A shadow of its former self, the delicate and delightful structure of the North Gate Refreshment Kiosk no longer functions as a bar and focal point for the gate on this side of the zoo. The bar counter itself (located on the line of the two recessed columns) has long since gone and the crispness of the canopy edge is compromised by over-felting. The sinusoidal shell nonetheless remains like an attenuated echo of the gaiety of a more innocent age.

Penguin Pool

1933–34
Listed Grade I

Lubetkin, Drake & Tecton

Lubetkin's celebrated *jeu d'esprit* proves the adage that monumentality may be quite independent of size. The Penguin Pool at London Zoo and its inhabitants have retained their admiring and affectionate audience, thanks to a substantial restoration carried out in the late 1980s with funding from English Heritage and private benefaction.

Perhaps not appreciated by the casual visitor is the integral relationship of the tree, a mature ailanthus, that pre-dates the Penguin Pool and attracted Lubetkin as a natural foil to his geometric abstraction. But the symbiosis is more than merely philosophical, as the falling twigs and foliage continue to provide the penguins with their nesting material.

The timber nesting-boxes lining the perimeter of the Penguin Pool at intervals are a result of the replacement of the original Antarctic penguins (which prefer to huddle in close quarters) by a species from South Africa that seeks more dispersed nesting sites. While these portable hutches might satisfy the conservation principle of 'reversibility', their appearance is nonetheless incongruous.

There was a joyful moment in the restoration project of 1987 when the penultimate layer of paint was removed to reveal the beautiful blue underside of the ramps, a detail that even Lubetkin had forgotten. Equally pleasing was the reinstatement of grey and red colouring around the perimeter promenade, in resemblance to the alternating quadrants of slate paviors and rubber compound originally installed to stimulate perambulation by the birds – the proof of which, unsurprisingly, remains inconclusive.

Whipsnade Park
Dunstable
Bedfordshire

Elephant House

1934–35
Listed Grade II*

Tecton

Perhaps more than any other single example in Lubetkin's zoological canon, the Elephant House at Whipsnade depended on the drama of its setting – a dense backdrop of mature evergreens roughly three times the height of the building itself. With the trees since cleared for access to a rear paddock, and an additional screen installed along the front edge of the bowstring canopy, the pavilion, though still impressive, has lost its classical metaphor and much of its tautness (compare with fig. 21, p. 20).

The Restaurant

1935

Lubetkin, Drake & Tecton

No longer the elegant eating place where, according to Lubetkin's recollection, diners would raise the sliding windows to offer titbits to the animals grazing outside, Whipsnade's restaurant is nonetheless still in beneficial use as a discovery centre enjoyed by youngsters and school parties.

Dudley Zoo
Castle Hill
Dudley
West Midlands

1935–37

Tecton

Sixty-five years after its spectacularly successful opening in 1937, Dudley Zoo lives on in a state of mild and melancholic oblivion. Like many zoos, it has faced the challenge of reinventing itself in an era of Disneyworld, themed experience and scepticism about the ethics of displaying captive animals. The Tecton buildings have been variously altered, neglected and, in the case of the Penguin Pool, demolished (see p. 141). Their settings have also changed dramatically as a result of a proliferation of ancillary structures and considerable reduction in the tree coverage. But in cases where the original buildings can be seen fairly unencumbered and survive relatively intact, such as the Bear Ravine, its adjacent kiosk and the hilltop Aviary, they retain a sort of elegiac grandeur reminiscent of some ancient site of Roman ruins. A complete scheme for the zoo's restoration and reuse prepared by Avanti Architects and approved by Lubetkin a few months before his death in 1990 remains on the shelf, awaiting implementation.

Kiosk 1
Listed Grade II*

Kiosk 2
Listed Grade II*

Though they have long since ceased to operate as kiosks dispensing chocolate and cigarettes, even the surviving shells of kiosks 1 and 2 at Dudley (below), lacking their lattice screens and appearing more like eighteenth-century follies, still retain the energy of Lubetkin's diametric composition.

Entrance Building
Listed Grade II

The clarion signage and exuberant stepped canopies of the entrance building (opposite) – an inventive response to the sloping site – still pack a punch in announcing the zoo's presence as one arrives in Dudley. But unless or until the attraction revives, the battery of ticket booths and turnstiles will seem like over-provision.

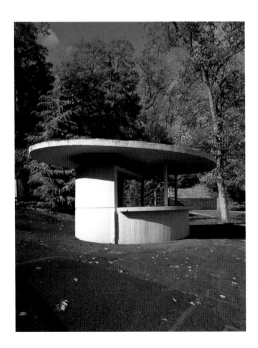

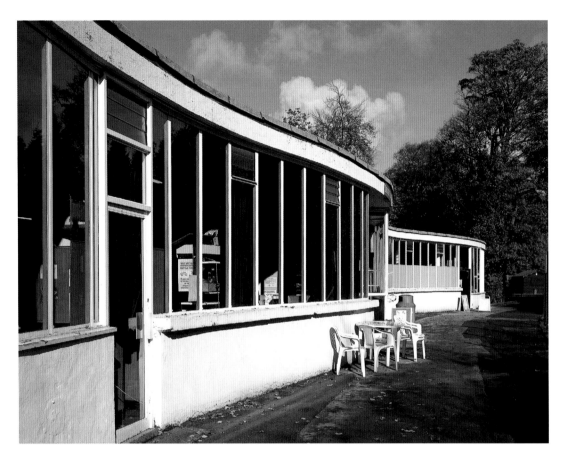

Moat Café
Listed Grade II

Originally open to the elements, with its serpentine roof hovering alongside the castle moat, the Moat Café at Dudley has been enclosed and converted for use as an education and exhibition centre. While this probably secured its survival, the solidity imparted by glazing right up to the canopy edge has all but erased the building's original identity.

Castle Restaurant
Listed Grade II

The popularity of this restaurant as an occasional venue for receptions and functions has also led to a process of incremental change and accretion, obliterating most of the building's authenticity. Nonetheless, its social use and its axial relationship to the castle still give it validity as one of the Tecton set.

Polar Bear Pit
Listed Grade II*

The Polar Bear Pit, most theatrical of all the Dudley exhibits, has long since ceased to house the species, now regarded as unsuitable for captive display. Its powerful form has also been somewhat compromised by zoo licensing legislation and the addition of metal barrier fencing. Doubtless safety must come first, but the proliferation of posts and wires obscures the simplicity of Tecton's ingenious parapet detail, which allowed children to look under, and adults to lean on, the generous perimeter rail.

Bear Ravine
Listed Grade II*

With its elevated gallery and commanding
views out over the Midlands industrial
plain, the old Bear Ravine at Dudley has
lost nothing of its grandeur despite the
departure of its original occupants and the
taming of the ravine itself into a grassed
paddock. The empty splendour of, and
restricted access to, this heroic structure
seems to encapsulate the predicament of
Dudley Zoo as whole.

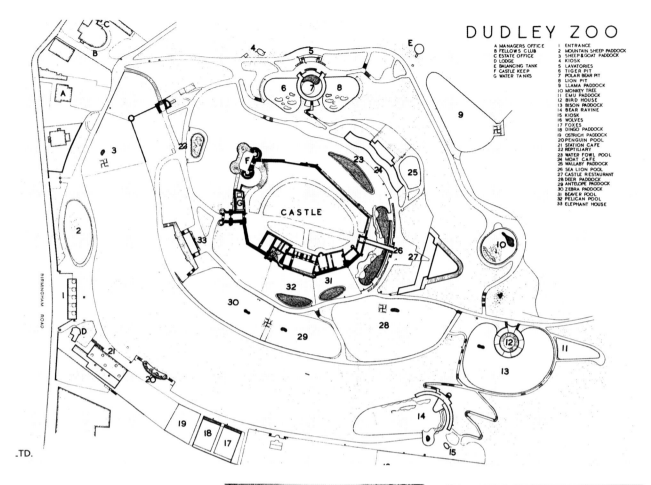

DUDLEY ZOO

A MANAGERS OFFICE
B FELLOWS CLUB
C ESTATE OFFICE
D LODGE
E BALANCING TANK
F CASTLE KEEP
G WATER TANKS

1 ENTRANCE
2 MOUNTAIN SHEEP PADDOCK
3 SHEEP & GOAT PADDOCK
4 KIOSK
5 LAVATORIES
6 TIGER PIT
7 POLAR BEAR PIT
8 LION PIT
9 LLAMA PADDOCK
10 MONKEY TREE
11 EMU PADDOCK
12 BIRD HOUSE
13 BISON PADDOCK
14 BEAR RAVINE
15 KIOSK
16 WOLVES
17 FOXES
18 DINGO PADDOCK
19 OSTRICH PADDOCK
20 PENGUIN POOL
21 STATION CAFE
22 REPTILIARY
23 WATER FOWL POOL
24 MOAT CAFE
25 WALLABY PADDOCK
26 SEA LION POOL
27 CASTLE RESTAURANT
28 DEER PADDOCK
29 ANTELOPE PADDOCK
30 ZEBRA PADDOCK
31 BEAVER POOL
32 PELICAN POOL
33 ELEPHANT HOUSE

Site plan

Tecton's original layout shows the orbital route system and siting of buildings to suit the difficult terrain. (The hairpin pathways connecting the Aviary and Bear Ravine give an indication of the gradients; see also fig. 24, p. 22.) Tecton's thirteen buildings (now twelve, with the loss of the Penguin Pool, 20) are outnumbered by additional structures. (The Station Café, 21, Reptiliary, 22, and Sea Lion Pool, 26, did not yield worthwhile survey images.)

Aviary
Listed Grade II*

Another of Lubetkin's circular plans, the fine listed structure of the Aviary at Dudley Zoo, placed to advantage on the ridge of Castle Hill (location 12 on site plan, above), assumes the significance of an eighteenth-century garden temple – a modern Stourhead perhaps, or a reprise of Pavlovsk by Charles Cameron, one of Lubetkin's heroes.

Elephant House
Listed Grade II

Ingeniously dug into the hillside to avoid impinging on views of the castle and to provide a terrace with high-level viewing of the animals, the Elephant House at Dudley Zoo – the second of three elephant houses that Tecton designed in the 1930s (see figs. 18 and 21, p. 20) – now has a forlorn look. The screen on the edge of the overhang is a later addition and a consequence of the building's exposed location. Sundry other modifications make this design, though clearly a member of the Dudley group, appear less significant than it really is.

**25, avenue de Versailles
Paris 16**

1928–31

Lubetkin & J. Ginsberg

It requires an intense effort of imagination to realize that this outstanding building, contemporaneous with Le Corbusier's Villa Savoye at Poissy, is now seventy years old and the debut project of two designers still in their twenties. The apartment block at 25, avenue de Versailles now seems almost dateless, so easy is its assimilation into the modern Paris street scene.

Some changes have nevertheless slightly lessened the building's authentic purity: the crushed-marble render of the façade, originally the colour of Bath stone, is now painted cream, as are the balcony walls, which originally were pale blue. The central column and undercroft are no longer in contrasting chocolate brown. The upper-level terraces have been enclosed with windscreening, and several windows have been replaced by unmatched substitutes. The infill glazing to the first-floor balcony is especially regrettable. It takes very little to spoil a façade of such impeccable resolution, and vigilance is needed to prevent further lapses into architectural amnesia.

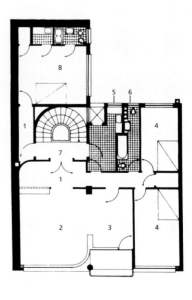

Key

1. Hall
2. Living-room
3. Dining-room
4. Bedroom
5. Kitchen
6. Bathroom
7. Stair/lift
8. Studio flat

It is the depth of modelling that proclaims the architects' maturity of judgement. Less confident designers would surely have mounted the windows nearer the building's edge in a bid to appear more 'modern' **(opposite)**.

The original bronze doors **(top right)** glow from refinement and decades of polishing, amply vindicating the architects' wisdom in specifying the best in the location of greatest use. The same priority would be accorded to the doors at Highpoint and Finsbury Health Centre.

The completion date and architects' names, albeit with some letters lost, remain where they left them **(bottom right)**, as if to prove their precocious authorship to the incredulous visitor. The desirability of these apartments surely puts the survival of this wonderful building beyond any foreseeable danger.

Highpoint I
North Hill
London N6

1933–35
Listed Grade I

Lubetkin & Tecton

Over sixty years on, the glimpse of
Highpoint I's unmistakable profile over
the tree tops **(above)** is still a thrilling sight
to any Modern Movement devotee. Though
the concrete parapet rail has been replaced
in aluminium, and the ubiquitous lightning
tapes offend the purist, the essentials of
green foliage, white architecture and blue
sky remain as compelling as on day one.

Many observers will be unaware that
one of the more prominent features of
Highpoint I, the lattice screens at the
junction of the spine and wings **(opposite)**,
is not original. These internal corners,
originally designed with horizontal railings
(like those at the balcony ends) and
intended for use as open drying areas,
were, however, too valuable as floorspace
not to be soon enclosed and incorporated
into the apartments themselves.

"The ground floor extends like the magnificent surface of a lake," wrote Le Corbusier after visiting Highpoint in 1935. The foyer, with its clean lines, lattice glazing and original light fittings, remains a definitive 1930s space. But it is invariably underpopulated, revealing the disparity between Lubetkin's Constructivist aspirations for a 'social condenser' and the reality of a bourgeois condominium.

Other than the fact that it came first, what makes Highpoint I different from a thousand white apartment blocks from Sydney to San Francisco is Lubetkin's unerring architectural judgement and the Englishness of its setting. The dark window frames leave the façades to read as an abstract statement of planes and cut-outs, the balcony fronts with their lyrical shadows providing a single counter-motif. One has only to visualize the consequences of, say, painting the window frames white, or extending the balconies beyond the window openings or giving the balconies themselves solid ends, to appreciate how crucial is Lubetkin's discipline to the overall sense of lightness and precision. At the time Highpoint I was built the adjacent site of Highpoint II was still a separate property, and therefore blank side gables were required. Yet Lubetkin insisted that, even had this not been a given, he would have refrained from introducing openings in these walls and thereby diminishing the contrast of the block's spartan clarity with its luscious garden setting.

The virtuoso flourish that completes Highpoint's *promenade architecturale* **(above)** was for Lubetkin a vital philosophical statement representing, in artistic terms, the interaction of causality and chance. But though consequently the staircase is also decidedly tricky for anyone of unsure footing, the precautionary handrail that has been added could surely have been more sympathetically conceived. It is another example of how buildings dependent on consistency of design for their aesthetic integrity need particular care and imagination when the demands of a later era are imposed.

(Opposite, clockwise from top left) Graciousness in miniature. Despite its modest dimensions, the double-width entrance conveys a sense of generosity, enhanced by the expressed oval column on the structural centre axis. "Like a Greek column," judged Sir Geoffrey Jellicoe, "this gives significance to the space in which it stands."

The ambitious concertina windows still function, albeit with effort, to create the open-air connection that Lubetkin intended. The ranging horizontal proportions of the opening serve to enlarge the perceived size of the room.

The lattice screen ingeniously transmits borrowed light to the communal landing beyond. But the rooms from which the light is borrowed are a later enclosure of the originally open drying balconies at block intersections (see also illustration, p. 85).

The shallow, built-in bedroom cupboards neatly conceal the spine beam while providing valuable storage with trombone slide-out clothes rails.

(Below) Detailed study of the smaller of the two main flat types shows the beautiful clarity of Lubetkin's planning.

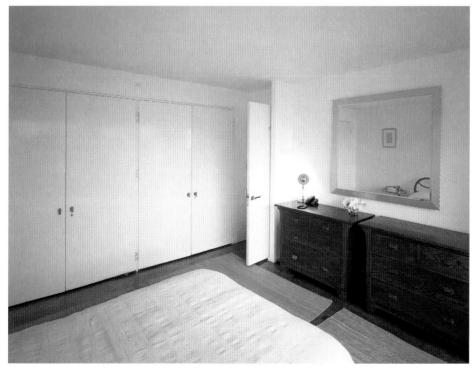

On a bright summer morning under a blue sky, trees in fresh leaf, tennis courts swept and ready, shadows perfectly obeying the laws of sciagraphy, the proposition represented by the Highpoint ensemble is surely irresistible – compact and convivial living in an Arcadian landscape twenty minutes from town. Little wonder this vision touched the heart of so many architects. But its enduring success depends on a vital 'ecosystem' of moderate density, adequate privacy, ample services, effective management and consistent maintenance. The neglect of such essentials explains the gulf between Highpoint's apotheosis of modernity and the brutalized inheritance of so many post-war housing estates. The familiarity of failure should not, however, obscure the validity of the ideal when properly applied, and Highpoint remains the first and still the most compelling vindication of Le Corbusier's vision of the 'vertical garden city' ever achieved in England.

Highpoint II
North Hill
London N6

1935–38
Listed Grade I

Lubetkin & Tecton

"It will bend, but it won't break," Ove Arup allegedly remarked after weighing up the feasibility of the massive cantilever Lubetkin proposed for Highpoint II's *porte cochère*. So indeed it has proved **(below)**. But at least the other change is reversible – that is, the emaciated lettering that replaced the original full-bodied signage in Thorne Shaded typeface, detailed by Peter Moro, Lubetkin's young assistant at the time (see fig. 39, p. 31).

The famous entrance of Highpoint II is familiar to countless Londoners who know nothing of Lubetkin. The façade of this once controversial building, with its varied materials and eclectic expression, is, however, timeless in a way that Highpoint I is not. Seen through the luscious foliage of its foreground, Highpoint II brings a European, indeed Mediterranean, ambience to its largely Victorian entourage. Yet such is the sense of Modernism at ease with itself that it is difficult now to imagine Highgate village without it.

With their double-height voids and spectacular views, the duplex units at Highpoint II took modern apartment living to new levels of style and opulence **(left)**. The aedicular doorway, given exactly the same proportional ratio as the opening in which it stands, provides the scaling element against which the grandeur of the saloon may be read, internally and externally (see also illustration, p. 97). Lubetkin's essay in luxury flats was nothing if not controversial among the more earnest socialist architects of the time, but he played the hand he was dealt with all the panache it deserved. Following 25, avenue de Versailles and Highpoint I, it was his third and last experience of designing private apartments, and these few splendid flats would soon be vastly outnumbered by the post-war social-housing schemes for which they provided such crucial technical grounding.

Another masterly staircase graces the interior of the central duplex flats at Highpoint II **(opposite)**. Finished in travertine and terrazzo and lined with Tecton's 'patent' oval handrail, these elements have a quiet elegance that was equalled only by Patrick Gwynne's staircase at The Homewood, Esher, Surrey, of the same date.

The children's paddling-pond **(above)** adjacent to the swimming-pool at Highpoint II, for years used merely as a tiered planter, has at last been rescued and repaired to provide a joyful embellishment to the gardens.

With both blocks now listed Grade I, Highpoint II may at last, and justly, share the limelight with its more celebrated forerunner. Siblings but not rivals, the two buildings need each other to narrate Lubetkin's – and the Modern Movement's – architectural development over the 1930s. From monolithic sculpture to articulate assembly, from Corbusier to Perret, the progression from early International Style conventions to the more complex reality of contemporary building represented by the second Highpoint block set the architectural agenda for the next twenty years and demonstrated the vast potentialities of Modernism for an oncoming generation of post-war architects. The planning authority's development restrictions served only to intensify Lubetkin's search for new solutions to the architectural questions he had just answered. Highpoint II adopts the same cornice line and window module as its neighbour but in all other respects employs another vocabulary – brick infill, tiled panels, expressed frame, floating balconies. Yet the compatibility of the two buildings proves the principle that the best townscape is not achieved by cloning but by intelligent differentiation.

"To dine out at Highpoint I, to arrive past the caryatids of Highpoint II just when the dark foliage is catching the lights, is still an architectural experience. For an Englishman it is, very nearly, to recapture some half-forgotten evening in some indefinable south; it is – as Henry James might have put it – 'to be so ineffably abroad'." Robert Furneaux Jordan, 1955

The Penthouse, Highpoint II

Considering the iconic status of the penthouse as Lubetkin's personal domestic testament, it seems incredible that as recently as the mid-1990s this unique apartment had fallen into a state of utter dereliction. However, after a rescue project by the late Michael Lamb and Avanti Architects to secure the building's fabric, new owners – painter Erez Yardeni and designer Ou Balyhodin – have made its complete refurnishing and ongoing conservation their life mission.

Though the roof of the penthouse required repair after years of water ingress, the characterful timber panelling **(right)** specified by Lubetkin had largely survived, missing pieces being made good with matching replacements. The vaulted ceiling brings spaciousness to the centre of the plan while minimizing the view of the roofline from the street. It is, however, the sliver of light that reveals Lubetkin's genius in transforming something solid into a link with the sky.

The use of Benjamin Pollock's theatrical prints as wallpaper **(above left)** might seem a quirky, decorative gesture, but they were really a surrogate for another, older form of figurative art from Lubetkin's past that remained dear to his heart – the ancient folk tradition of the *lubki*, handmade woodcuts flyposted on village walls and a sort of *lingua franca* among the illiterate peasantry of old Russia. Here the prints' exact reinstatement has been achieved by meticulous scrutiny of original photographs and the conscientious assistance of Pollock's Toy Museum in London. Note also Lubetkin's distinctive two-by-two tile grid, giving the floorscape the scale he desired.

From outside to inside to outside **(above right)**, this view sums up the intended sense of connection between internal spaces and the *toit jardin*. With typical ingenuity Lubetkin arranged for the two bed covers to be made to exactly the size of the glazed doors in order to serve as curtains at night time.

The concrete mantelpiece **(below left)**, recast in replica as part of the rescue project to replace the missing original, was possibly the first architectural use of boardmarked shuttering in England. Unquestionably unique was Lubetkin's door embellishment with enlarged images of plankton and marine life – another lost feature of the penthouse now re-created by painstaking computer graphics.

Most architects would have given the garden view to this, the main bedroom of the penthouse **(below right)**. But Lubetkin, realizing that panorama was the exclusive claim of the living space, made the more subtle decision to glaze the sides. This leaves the end wall to echo the vaulted roof shape on plan, and to provide a blue background against which the Eames chaise longue floats like a white cloud.

With the reconstruction of the bookshelves against their claret background, the replication of the deep-pile rug interlaced with ribbons in alternate colours, the relining of the door and the return of Lubetkin's original furniture, the penthouse is gradually recapturing its authenticity **(opposite)**. Yet such is its cultural inclusiveness that the tastes of the current owners have also been absorbed without incongruity.

The glimpse of light through glass blocks in the bookshelf ends in the penthouse at Highpoint II is another detail revealing Lubetkin's acute sensibilities. Now it only remains to rebuild the console screen to complete the re-creation of this transcendent space. A Japanese visitor recently described the penthouse as belonging to another planet, suspended halfway between the earth and the moon.

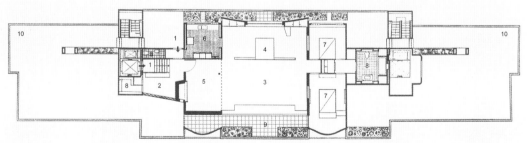

Key

1. Entrance
2. Hallway
3. Living area
4. Dining area
5. Fireside
6. Kitchen
7. Bedroom
8. Bathroom/Cloakroom
9. Terrace
10. Block outline

The well-worn Corbusian comparison of modern buildings and ocean liners does less than full justice to the view of the Highpoint ensemble across the verdant playing fields of Highgate School. Sir Geoffrey Jellicoe, the great landscape architect, who in his later years came to Highpoint from a nearby Georgian terrace, placed Lubetkin's design and its incomparable setting in historical perspective and was in no doubt that he had "moved from static Roman thought into creative Greek thought". His insight reminds us that the image of these apartments rising above the greenery of their foreground is not just a twentieth-century view in north London; it is also a classical vision of man's ideal place in the world.

Finsbury Health Centre
Pine Street
London E1

1935–38
Listed Grade I

Tecton

A smiling façade, a brave nameplate and a small green oasis mark the architectural birthplace of the British Welfare State. The foreground gardens of the Finsbury Health Centre were originally to extend to Farringdon Road. This would have given the building a setting befitting its importance and axial presentation. Alas, this planning vision was not pursued and now the most significant example of modern social architecture of the inter-war period lies hidden behind a wretched terrace of Post-modern houses and a gross multi-storey car park.

First-time visitors who know the Finsbury Health Centre only through photographs are invariably surprised by how small it is. This is really an acknowledgement of Lubetkin's way of endowing his works with monumentality – in this instance partly by symmetry, but also through the sense of ceremony associated with its access (top left).

The partial restoration of the building in the mid-1990s by Camden & Islington NHS Trust with Avanti Architects retrieves the richness of the curtain walling and the original colours (bottom left), but also highlights the dire urgency of finding the funds and the will to tackle the remainder.

The rear elevation and service courtyard (above right), for which funds were not available in the 1994 restoration project, remain in forlorn condition, the curtain wall languishing with damaged windows and substitute panels, glass blockwork in urgent need of repair and the original concrete colours blandly overpainted. If Grade I listing counts for anything it must surely underscore the priority of Finsbury's claim for help.

Gordon Cullen's uplifting murals have sadly succumbed to the NHS nostrum, "if it doesn't move, stick a notice on it". Other changes include the floor finish (covering the original three-by-three tile grid), the colour scheme, lost photomurals on the sculpted wall and the large reception desk **(above)**. But even billboard psoriasis, anarchic wiring, crass light fittings and serried seating cannot obliterate the essential order and humanity of this pivotal space, lit by its gently curving glass-block wall (compare with fig. 43, p. 34).

Now we are used to the modern hospital corridor, the passages at Finsbury **(right)** may seem unremarkable until you remember the overcrowded, soot-covered, rat-infested environs at the time it was built. The invasive radiators and pipework, visual intrusions that Lubetkin would find intolerable, are more recent and quite contradict the logic of the exterior ducts.

Spa Green
Rosebery Avenue/St John Street
London EC1

1943–50
Listed Grade II*

Tecton; executive architects
Skinner & Lubetkin

Rightly listed, the first and best of Lubetkin and Tecton's post-war housing schemes set a standard in architectural and technical accomplishment unmatched by any contemporary. Over half a century later Spa Green still radiates a sense of optimism that defies the commonplace dismissal of flatted estates as a modern urban aberration.

Close scrutiny of Spa Green's façades shows how their rich architectural effects are achieved by simple material detailing **(below)**. A measure of subtlety has been lost by painting all the balcony elements in Indian red, whereas originally only the divider walls and columns were in this colour, while the grilles and back walls were slate grey. Such bespoke elements as the canopy, however, retain Lubetkin's authentic signature.

Spa Green shows how Lubetkin's sense of proportion and façade composition was adapted to the challenge of large post-war blocks. His insistence that an elevation had civic obligations beyond the internal planning it enclosed is evident here **(opposite)** in the way the central tiled frame is widened to contain a double stack of windows, thereby centring the composition, when in fact the left-hand set belong to the flats outside the frame.

SADLER HOUSE

(Opposite) Retiled and refurbished in the 1980s, the buildings stand in generally good order, but require ongoing care and commitment to remain so. Telltale signs of Right-to-Buy legislation are becoming evident in the sporadic window alterations. Understandable though this is, the challenge is to adopt a standard replacement or organize repairs collectively, regardless of tenure, if visual anarchy is to be avoided.

Lucienne (below left), one of Spa Green's most ardent supporters, enjoys the relationship between the kitchen (where she is standing) and the living-room. Tecton's interest in every detail of compact domestic living gives the units an enduring practicality.

The living-room's direct connection to the third bedroom (below right) allows this to function as a study or office, and enhances the plan's responsiveness to changing lifestyles. The fireplace reveals Lubetkin's attachment to the canted frame, a motif traceable through the restaurant at Whipsnade and Finsbury Health Centre (see illustrations, pp. 73 and 104)

The rear of Sadler House, arguably the most distinguished public-sector gallery-access housing block in England. The later addition of this solid tower (right), from the circular landing at first-floor level, though introducing a discordant 1930s note, does not impair the sensuous dynamic of this outstanding building.

Priory Green
Collier Street
London N1

1943–52

Tecton; executive architects
Skinner, Bailey & Lubetkin

After years of insufficient care and support
this monument of early post-war housing
is now set for substantial refurbishment
by the Peabody Trust, thanks to its
designation as a Conservation Area and
the consequential award of a £2 million
Heritage Lottery grant. Concrete repair,
retiling, window renewal, proper security
measures and comprehensive re-landscaping
should bring this essentially viable and
architecturally significant housing to a
condition fit for an extended future.

The large blocks at Priory Green present
one of Lubetkin's most vigorously modelled
façade designs **(below left)**, which
maintain their identity despite various
service accretions and material wear and
tear. The original cast-iron latticework of
rainwater pipes has been replaced in steel,
but this feature still delineates the forceful
geometry of the façade.

With its considerable green area and tree
coverage, the large central space **(below
right)** has effectively become a private park.
The proposed regeneration will reconfigure
the landscaping along the lines of Tecton's
original design, improving access, security
and amenity.

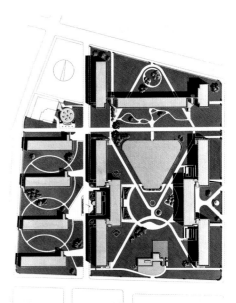

**Priory Green Extension
(now Priory Heights)
Wynford Road
London N1**

1946–57

**Tecton; development and
execution Skinner, Bailey
& Lubetkin**

Originally Priory Green's second phase
and poor relation, Wynford House, now
renamed Priory Heights, has undergone
major regeneration in an award-winning
project by the Community Housing
Association and Avanti Architects.
Reopened in 2000 as a mixed-tenure
social and private rental estate, the three
blocks have been modified, repaired and
re-serviced, with new penthouses replacing
redundant rooftop tankrooms.

A new porch and concierge point **(below
left)** has been configured from the original
staircase lobby, allowing improved access
at ground level and introducing toplight
through a new cockpit. The new doorway
and canopy acknowledge the Lubetkin
tradition of ceremonious entrances.

The landscaping **(below right)** has been
reconfigured to improve access and
security, but incorporates the motif of
a circular garden intended in Lubetkin's
original design but lost in budget cuts.
The picture shows the new layout before
completion of planting.

The old, and latterly disused, tenants' meeting rooms have been restored and converted to provide a new children's play facility. The charming concrete low relief **(opposite)** above the main hall has been cleaned and restored to become, with its semi-abstract portrait of a family group, a fitting emblem for the centre.

Concrete repair was tackled as a conservation task, avoiding overcladding and blanket coatings, and seeking instead to reinstate the vigorous contrasts of Lubetkin's original façade composition. Windows have been replaced to the original fenestration patterns, but to current performance standards. Retiling has been undertaken using matching tiles, adopting the original bay-joint module.

Removal of the bridge links between blocks and reconstruction of the staircases as independent escapes have improved security and allow sunshine to penetrate the north-facing courtyard **(below right)**.

**Bevin Court
Cruikshank Street
London WC1**

**1946–54
Listed Grade II**

**Tecton; development and
execution Skinner, Bailey &
Lubetkin**

Though the scheme as built was conceived
as a more economic alternative to the
original proposal to re-create Holford
Square in a modern idiom, the triaxial
block has such a powerful identity
(opposite), both in its physical context
and, indeed, in the whole Lubetkin canon,
as to avoid any sense of compromise.

The Lenin connection (see pp. 39 and 141)
was originally to have provided the block's
name, but in the changed circumstances of
the eventual project it was superseded by
that of Foreign Secretary Ernest Bevin – a
volte-face that, in Francis Skinner's ironic
account of the signage design, required the
substitution of only two letters **(top right)**.

Holford House **(middle left)**, though
arguably upstaged by Bevin Court,
nevertheless plays a crucial part in linking
the overall composition to Percy Circus, of
which it forms a section while echoing the
splayed geometry of the larger block (see
fig. 59, p. 42).

Bevin Court's later companion **(middle
right)** lies alongside its listed neighbour
in discreet anonymity, now typically spoilt
by errant cables, thoughtless grilles and
bodged plumbing. Amwell House does
not purport to be great architecture but
it deserves its share of informed care.

Located in the original position of the
porter's lodge, which itself was intended
to overlook the relocated Lenin Memorial,
Peter Yates's fine mural of London signs
and symbols **(bottom right)** would benefit
from a little TLC. Significantly, however, it
has never been vandalized.

Even the view **(below left)** from the entrance hallway hardly prepares the first-time visitor for the revelation of the staircase. But on reaching the edge of the ceiling circle **(opposite)** the sensation is revealed. It is difficult to cite any public staircase in the whole Modern Movement that can rival Lubetkin's masterpiece at Bevin Court. Though the original colours have gone, its spatial potency remains undiminished.

The triaxial plan form of the building becomes the stair motif itself in two half flights per floor **(top left)**, meeting and leaving the triangular landings and rotated at each level towards a different London panorama. Lubetkin's conception gathers and sublimates all the geometric energy of its urban surroundings.

Hallfield
Bishop's Bridge Road
London W2

1946–54

Tecton; development and
execution Drake & Lasdun

Lubetkin to Lasdun: a new formality. Hallfield marks the great baton change of British architecture, from second- to third-generation high Modernism. Lubetkin's building carries Lasdun's balconies **(opposite)**, which surely foreshadow that twisted geometry soon to be deployed in the lecture theatre at the Royal College of Physicians, London.

Not maisonettes, but flats. The balconies suggest a duplex section, but in fact are used only as an elevational device to decorate alternate levels in a block of identical plans **(above left)**.

Lubetkin's chequer motif is here refined to its very essence – expressed not as mechanical repetition but as a lively dynamic **(above right)**. Every component has its place as part of a larger composite, which in turn builds the hierarchy of scale to the overall ensemble. A further enrichment, the alternating bands of brickwork colour, was Lasdun's idea.

Majestic, creamy and robust, the blocks of Hallfield **(opposite)** are worthy neighbours of their Bayswater terraces. Indeed, given hindsight's knowledge of housing idioms that came after, it is difficult now to imagine any period of British architecture since the War that could have produced a more appropriate response to this distinctive tract of London townscape.

The key residential essentials – space, order and good light – are revealed in this inviting glimpse of a living-room interior in Hallfield's Pembroke House **(right)**.

A gentle reminder that alongside all Lubetkin's theorizing and philosophy the practical tasks of design and construction went on **(below left)**. The more often a detail is repeated, he would say, the more important it is for it to be fully resolved.

Well-proportioned and easily furnished, the bedrooms **(below right)** have a timeless quality that makes them feel both modern and dateless.

Dorset Estate
Diss Street/Ravenscroft Street
London E2

1951–57

Skinner, Bailey & Lubetkin

A comparative glance at Spa Green less than a decade earlier shows the extent to which increasing bureaucracy, budget restraints and numerical targets had altered the culture of British public-sector housing. Skinner, Bailey and Lubetkin's large but difficult first essay for the Metropolitan Borough of Bethnal Green lost much of its urban logic when the site frontage to Hackney Road could not be secured, and the required accommodation was perforce concentrated into two dense backland blocks. The lack of modelling on the buildings themselves was not helped by the substitution of Kentish Ragstone aggregate panels for tile cladding, reducing the intended contrasts. The façade illustrated nevertheless shows how the chequer device imparts consistency across adjacent elevations **(below left)**, where one comprises dwelling units and the other access galleries.

A refurbishment project in the 1980s improved the buildings significantly with fabric repairs, cleaning and painting of the panel edges. This estate speaks of its time, and yet its austerity has a certain quiet dignity **(below right)** when considering the Post-modern excesses that would follow.

Hidden in the core of the two main blocks stands a pair of staircase gems **(opposite)**. This design inverts the radial solution at Bevin Court, with a series of orbital half flights rotating within the hexagonal floor landings. The upward view, with its implication of man's spiral ascent, provides another echo of Lubetkin's Constructivist background.

Community Centre and Library

The Community Centre and Library building, symbolically placed at the fulcrum of the estate, has been much altered by the outward extension of the ground floor (originally recessed below the upper level) and addition of the familiar security paraphernalia of today's troubled world. But it remains in beneficial use and still belongs in the Lubetkin canon of circular buildings, his favourite plan figure.

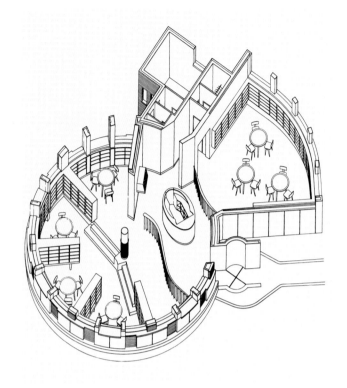

The Victoria

The traditional East End pub is gently
modernized in this adjunct to one of the
four-storey maisonette blocks at Dorset
Estate. Modern Movement pilgrims will
find no evidence of Lubetkin inside, but
the drink still flows.

Shipton Street

This simple three-storey block was
Lubetkin's first use of the terrace form
since Genesta Road some twenty years
earlier (see pp. 54–55). Only the fenestration
pattern, albeit in replacement windows,
with its alternating rows of toplights and
sublights on first and second floors,
provides the clue to authorship of this
modest and workmanlike frontage.

Sivill House
Columbia Road
London E2

1960–64

Skinner, Bailey & Lubetkin

The London County Council demanded a twenty-storey point block, and the architects delivered **(below left)**. This landmark of east London, neatly planned with four units per floor in hinged and finely mitred stacks, remains in good order, with a rugged elegance and assertive identity that distinguish it from a hundred other tower blocks of its time.

The main façade to Columbia Road reflects Lubetkin's ongoing search for visual energy in window composition and elements of construction. The characteristic cladding figure **(below right)** is an abstracted adaptation of the highly stylized dragon motif used in Caucasian carpets of the sixteenth and seventeenth centuries.

Detailed study **(opposite)** shows how, instead of simply adopting a single solution and repeating it, Lubetkin presents the choice itself as the 'reality', exploiting its permutations to animate the composition.

Lakeview
Old Ford Road
London E3

1953–56

Skinner, Bailey & Lubetkin

Even the tiny two-storey blocks **(below left)**, each containing two pairs of single-bedroom units, have an architectonic quality in their façade treatment and loggia that, together with the maroon tile motif, links them to the main building. Alas, visitations of the cabling and exterior pipework vandals are again in evidence.

The replacement windows lose some of the fineness and flexibility of the originals, which included top-hung lights in addition to the casements, but the whitened reveals and white frames help to brighten the façade in the absence of concrete cleaning.

The diagonal site organization **(opposite)**, Lubetkin's main contribution, reflects his desire to present the scheme as a gateway to Victoria Park. It is tempting to compare these blocks, with their bridge connections to a free-standing shared staircase, to Denys Lasdun's contemporaneous cluster-block scheme at nearby Usk Street for the same client, though Lasdun denied any such relationship. (See also fig. 70, p. 47.)

Cranbrook
Roman Road
London E2

1955–65

Skinner, Bailey & Lubetkin

The grandeur of Lubetkin's overall design (see fig. 72, p. 48) presents a powerful geometric composition when viewed from the flats above, but is not sustained at ground level **(right)**. Though original poplars along the diagonal avenue remain, the estate as a whole needs an upgraded landscape treatment to improve the external ambience and match its architectural scale.

The inevitable security measures and entryphones **(below left)** have changed the open character of the entrance hallways but are readily absorbed by the strength of the original design.

Were it not for such details as the concrete hoppers and canted eaves, many might not recognize these modest bungalows **(below right)** as the work of the architects of Highpoint and Finsbury Health Centre. But the humane sanctuary of the old-people's housing enclave vindicates the original design decision to group these units together around their own garden, where a focus is provided by Elisabeth Frink's distinctive statuette *The Blind Beggar of Bethnal Green*, now listed Grade II*.

The façades **(below left)** retain their restless flickering, though the windows and spandrel panels have all been replaced, as have also the green boxes (originally concrete panels) that 'contour' the blocks at two-storey intervals. The consequences of renewing gas supplies with external pipework are all too apparent.

A teardrop motif informs the penultimate in the series of Lubetkin's fine staircases **(below right)**. The upward view still conveys its drama, only slightly reduced by the loss of strongly contrasting paintwork on the slab edges.

**Butterick Factory
Leigh Park
Havant
Hampshire**

1954–57

Skinner, Bailey & Lubetkin

This businesslike scheme for the American pattern company continues in beneficial use, with altered windows and the roadside block now rendered.

**Tabard Garden Estate
Tabard Street
Southwark
London SE1**

c. 1962–65

Skinner, Bailey & Lubetkin

A little-known part of the larger London County Council estate in Southwark, south-east London, now due for regeneration.

**Club 85
Whinbush Road
Hitchin
Hertfordshire**

c. 1965–68

Skinner, Bailey & Lubetkin; executive architects Skinner & Bailey

Defensively boarded where once generously glazed, this working-men's club now has a melancholic air. Even its originally landscaped foreground has been reduced to parking tarmac.

St Andrew's Ambulance Association
Milton Street
Cowcaddens
Glasgow

c. 1966–70

Skinner, Bailey & Lubetkin

The bold St Andrew's cross motif and the
dramatic design of the public staircase were
Lubetkin's contributions to this project by
his Scottish partner Douglas Bailey.

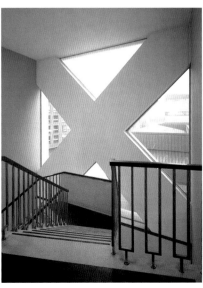

Beaux Arts interpretation it is also a display, it is a dance ..." Lubetkin, 1975

Club Trapèze Volant
rue des Volontaires
Paris 15

Built 1927
Dismantled c. 1938

USSR Trades Demountable Exhibition Pavilion
used in Bordeaux, Marseille, Nancy, Tours, Strasbourg

First opened c. 1928
Last used 1931

Venesta Display Stand
The Building Exhibition
London

Built and dismantled 1934

Shelter
Whipsnade Park
Dunstable
Bedfordshire

Built 1934
Demolished early 1950s

Giraffe House
Whipsnade Park
Dunstable
Bedfordshire

Built 1934–35, since modified and largely demolished

Gestetner Factory
Fawley Road/Broad Lane
London N15

**Extensions and
modifications 1935–50
Demolished 1980s**

Penguin Pool
Dudley Zoo
Castle Hill, Dudley
West Midlands

Built 1937
Listed Grade II
Demolished *c*. 1979

Studio of Animal Art
London Zoo
Regent's Park
London NW1

**Built 1936–37
Demolished 1962**

Lenin Memorial
Holford Square
London WC1

**Built 1942
Demolished 1951**

**Cranbrook *trompe
l'œil* sculpture**
Roman Road
London E2

**Built 1965
Largely destroyed by 1994**

Writings by Lubetkin

B. Lubetkin and J. Ginsberg, 'Comment concevez-vous la fenêtre?', *L'Architecture d'ajourd'hui*, no. 4, Paris 1931

B. Lubetkin, 'L'Architecture en Angleterre', *L'Architecture d'aujourd'hui*, no. 10, Paris 1932, pp. 2–23

B. Lubetkin, 'The Builders', *Architectural Review*, May 1932, pp. 201–14; reprinted in *Documents: A Collection of Source Material on the Modern Movement*, Milton Keynes (Open University Press) 1975

B. Lubetkin, 'Pages d'un journal du chantier', *Architectural Review*, October 1932, pp. 133–34

B. Lubetkin, 'Town and Landscape Planning in Soviet Russia', *Architectural Association Journal*, January 1933; reprinted in *Architectural Association 125th Special Commemorative Publication*, London (Professional Publications) 1973, pp. 145–53

B. Lubetkin, interview in *American Architect and Architecture*, December 1936, pp. 25–26

B. Lubetkin, 'Modern Architecture in England', *American Architect and Architecture*, February 1937, pp. 29–30

B. Lubetkin, 'Bungalows at Whipsnade', *Architectural Review*, vol. 81, 1937, p. 60

B. Lubetkin and Tecton, *Planned ARP*, London (Architectural Press) 1939

B. Lubetkin and L. Brett, 'Canons of Criticism', *Architectural Review*, March 1951, pp. 135–37

B. Lubetkin, 'Flats in Rosebery Avenue, Finsbury', *Architectural Review*, vol. 109, 1951, pp. 138–40

B. Lubetkin, 'Flats in Holford Square', *Architectural Review*, June 1952, pp. 403–06

B. Lubetkin, 'Soviet Architecture: Notes on Developments, 1917–1932', *Architectural Association Journal*, May 1956, pp. 260–64

B. Lubetkin, 'Soviet Architecture: Notes on Developments, 1932–1955', *Architectural Association Journal*, September–October 1956, pp. 85–89

B. Lubetkin, 'Art, Ideology and Revolution', Milton Keynes (Open University Press) 1975 (History of Architecture and Design, Unit A305/27)

B. Lubetkin, 'A Commentary on Western Architecture', Milton Keynes (Open University Press) 1975 (History of Architecture and Design, Unit A305/27)

B. Lubetkin, lecture to the Royal College of Art, London, 1976; see J. Allan and M. Reading, *The Writings of Berthold Lubetkin*, London (ARCUK) June 1989

B. Lubetkin, Royal Gold Medal address, 29 June 1982, reproduced in J. Allan, *Berthold Lubetkin: Architecture and the Tradition of Progress*, London (RIBA Publications) 1992, pp. 585–89

B. Lubetkin and J. Allan, The President's Invitation Lecture, *RIBA Transactions 8*, vol. 4, no. 2, 1986, pp. 4–11

Writings about Lubetkin and his work

J. Allan, *Berthold Lubetkin: Architecture and the Tradition of Progress*, London (RIBA Publications) 1992 (see Bibliography, pp. 604–09, and Directory of Works, pp. 590–599)

J. Allan, 'The Unattached Collaborator', *Architects' Journal*, 23 June 1982

J. Allan, 'Lubetkin and Peterlee', in *The Modern City Revisited*, ed. T. Deckker, London and New York (E. & F.N. Spon) 2000, pp. 103–24

T. Benton, 'Berthold Lubetkin e il sogno del modernismo', *Casabella*, 601, May 1993, pp. 46–51

P. Coe and M. Reading, *Lubetkin and Tecton: Architecture and Social Commitment*, Bristol (Arts Council of Great Britain and University of Bristol) 1981

W. Curtis, 'Berthold Lubetkin: Socialist Architecture in the Diaspora', *Architectural Association Quarterly*, vol. 8, no. 3, 1976, pp. 33–39

T. Diehl, 'Theory and Principle: Berthold Lubetkin's Highpoint One and Highpoint Two', *Journal of Architectural Education*, Cambridge MA (MIT Press for The Association of the Collegiate Schools of Architecture) May 1999, pp. 233–41

R. Furneaux Jordan, 'Lubetkin', *Architectural Review*, July 1955, pp. 36–54

S. Gardiner, 'Apostle of the Concrete Curve', *Observer*, 7 June 1981

P. Guillery, *The Buildings of London Zoo*, London (Royal Commission on the Historical Monuments of England) 1993

L. Kehoe, *In this Dark House*, New York (Schocken Books) 1995; London (Viking) 1996

J. Kerr, 'Lenin's Bust: Unlikely Allies in Wartime London', *Strangely Familiar*, London (Routledge) 1996

S. Lambert, 'Historic Pioneers: Architects and Clients', *Architects' Journal*, 11 March 1970

S. Lubetkin, 'Lubetkin: The Untold Story', *World Architecture 24*, London (Cheerman) 1993

P. Mardaga (ed.), *Berthold Lubetkin: Un moderne en Angleterre*, Brussels (Pierre Mardaga) 1983

C. Marti and J. Ros (eds.), *Berthold Lubetkin (1901–1990)*, Documents de Projectes d'Arquitectura, Escola d'Arquitectura de Barcelona, 1997

P. Moro, 'Building on Humour', *Architects' Journal*, 19 and 26 August 1992, pp. 50–51

G. Nelson, 'Architects of Europe Today, 12: Tecton, England', *Pencil Points*, October 1936, pp. 527–40

M. Reading and P. Coe, *Lubetkin and Tecton: An Architectural Study*, London (Triangle Architectural Publishing) 1992

A. Saint, 'Terrorist Tamed: The Fight and Flight of Berthold Lubetkin', *Times Literary Supplement*, 20 November 1992, pp. 5–6

D. Sharp, 'Reflecting Lubetkin', *Building*, 25 June 1982

W. Tatton-Brown, 'Lubetkin Honoured: Tecton Remembered', *Architects' Journal*, 23 June 1982, p. 35

Conservation of Lubetkin's works

J. Allan, 'Tectonic Icon Restored', *RIBA Journal*, February 1988, pp. 30–32

J. Allan, 'Landmark of the Thirties Restored', *Concrete Quarterly*, vol. 157, April–June 1988, pp. 2–5

J. Allan, 'Modern Theory of Repair', *Architects' Journal Renovation Supplement*, March 1989, pp. 18–21

J. Allan, 'Renovation: Tecton's Concrete at Dudley Zoo', *Architecture Today 13*, 1990, p. 91

J. Allan, 'Conservation of the Works of Lubetkin and Tecton, Architects', *Proceedings of the Docomomo First International Conference: Eindhoven University of Technology, 12–15 September 1990*, ed. H.-J. Henket and W. de Jonge, 1991, pp. 180–85

J. Allan, 'The Conservation of Modern Architecture', in *Building Maintenance and Preservation*, ed. Edward Mills, 2nd edn, London (Butterworth) 1994

J. Allan, 'Conservation of Modern Buildings: A Practitioner's View', in *Modern Matters*, ed. S. Macdonald, London (English Heritage/Donhead) 1996

J. Allan, 'MOMO's Second Chance: The Revaluation of Urban Housing', *Proceedings of the Docomomo Fifth International Conference: Stockholm, Swedish Museum of Architecture, 16–18 September 1998*, ed. M. Botta, pp. 102–104; full text reproduced in A. Cunningham (ed.), *Modern Movement Heritage*, London and New York (E. & F.N. Spon) 1998

J. Allan, 'A Tailored Remediation Strategy', in *The Fairface of Concrete*, ed. W. de Jonge and A. Doolaar, Eindhoven (Eindhoven University of Technology/Docomomo) 1998

J. Allan, 'Preserving Heritage or Revaluing Resources?', in *Preserving Post-war Heritage*, ed. S. Macdonald and K. Wedd, London (English Heritage/Donhead) 2001

K. Bateson, 'True to Form', *Building Design*, 17 November 2000, pp. 16–19

C. Davies, 'Prescription for a Health Centre', *Architects' Journal Renovation Supplement*, March 1989, pp. 12–17

M. Field, 'A Pioneer Partially Restored to its Former Glory', *Architects' Journal*, 16 February 1995, pp. 22–23

J. Glancey, 'A Vision Still Worth Fighting For', *Independent*, 29 March 1995

S. Macdonald, 'Long Live Modern Architecture', *The Modern House Revisited*, Journal of the Twentieth Century Society, no. 2, 1996

A. Mead, 'Modern Movement Classic on a Highgate Hilltop', *Architects' Journal*, 12 September 1996

H. Pearman, 'Re-doing it in Style', *Sunday Times*, 23 February 1992

M. Spring, 'Modern Medicine' *Building*, 5 December 1997

S. Trocme, 'Sticklers for Detail', *New York Times Magazine*, Fall 2000, pp. 96–100

Lubetkin obituaries
J. Allan, 'The Passing of a Modern Master', *Architects' Journal*, 31 October 1990

J. Allan, 'A Fighter on Two Fronts', *Architectural Review*, December 1990

J. Allan, 'Berthold Lubetkin: Pioneer Modernist', *RIBA Journal*, December 1990, pp. 30–32

'Berthold Lubetkin', *Daily Telegraph*, 25 October 1990

'Berthold Lubetkin', *The Times*, 24 October 1990

M. Gardiner, 'Berthold Lubetkin', *Independent*, 25 October 1990

S. Gardiner, 'Simple Reticence of an Inspired Journeyman', *Observer*, 28 October 1990

P. Moro, 'Berthold Lubetkin', *Architectural Review*, December 1990, p. 4

M. Pawley, 'A Modernist Master', *Guardian*, 24 October 1990

D. Sharp, 'Berthold Lubetkin', *Independent*, 25 October 1990

General and related titles
C. Benton, *A Different World: Emigré Architects in Britain, 1928–1958*, London (RIBA Heinz Gallery) 1995

W. Curtis, *Modern Architecture Since 1900*, 3rd edn, London (Phaidon Press) 1996, pp. 329–49

W. Curtis, *Denys Lasdun: Architecture, City, Landscape*, London (Phaidon Press) 1994

T. Dannatt, *Modern Architecture in Britain*, London (Batsford) 1959

D. Dean, *The Thirties: Recalling the English Architectural Scene*, London (Trefoil Books) 1983

L. Esher, *A Broken Wave: The Rebuilding of England, 1940–1980*, London (Allen Lane) 1981

K. Frampton, *Modern Architecture: A Critical History*, London (Thames & Hudson) 1980

H.R. Hitchcock, *Modern Architecture in England*, New York (Museum of Modern Art) 1937; reprinted New York (Arno Press) 1969

A. Jackson, *The Politics of Architecture*, London (Architectural Press) 1970

P. Morreau, *Ove Arup, 1895–1988*, London (Institution of Civil Engineers) 1995

A. Powers, 'The Search for a New Reality', in *Modern Britain, 1929–1939*, exhib. cat., ed. J. Peto and D. Loveday, London, Design Museum, 1999, p. 37

B. Riseboro, *Modern Architecture and Design: An Alternative History*, London (Herbert Press) 1982; Cambridge MA (MIT Press) 1983

F.R.S. Yorke and F. Gibberd, *The Modern Flat*, London (Architectural Press) 1937

Page numbers in *italic* refer to illustrations in the introductory essay. Page numbers in **bold** refer to main entries in the illustrated survey.

air-raid shelters 37–38, *37*
Amwell House, London 119
Architects and Technicians Organization (ATO) 33
Architectural Association 17
Arup, Ove 19–21, 27, 31, 36, 40, 63, 93
Avanti Architects 74, 98, 106, 114
Avenue de Versailles, Paris 14–16, *15, 16*, **80–83**

Bailey, Douglas 46, 137
Balyhodin, Ou 98
Bauhaus 12
Beach House, The, Aldwick Bay, West Sussex 22, *23*, **57**
Bernal, J.D. 17
Bethnal Green, Metropolitan Borough of 46–47
Bevin Court, London *42, 43*, **118–21**
Blum, — *16*
Breuer, Marcel 18
Busaco Street housing project, London *36, 37*, 42
Butterick Factory, Havant, Hampshire **136**

Calder, Alexander 33
Cameron, Charles 79
Cement Marketing Company *33*, 35
Chandigarh 46
Chermayeff, Serge 18
Chitty, Anthony 17, 57
Church, Margaret *see* Lubetkin, Margaret (née Church)
Churchill, Winston 37–38
Club 85, Hitchin, Hertfordshire **136**
Club Trapèze Volant, Paris 13, *15*, 140
Community Housing Association 114
Cranbrook, London 47–49, *48–49*, **134–35**, 141
Cullen, Gordon *34*, 36, 107

Dorset Estate, London *47*, **126–29**
Drake, Lindsay *17*
Drake & Lasdun 43, 123
Dudley Zoo, West Midlands *20*, 21–22, *22*, **74–79**, 141
  Aviary *22*, **79**
  Bear Ravine *22*, **78**
  Castle Restaurant **76**
  Elephant House **79**
  Entrance Building *20*, **74–75**
  Kiosks *22*, **74**
  Moat Café **76**
  Penguin Pool 141
  Polar Bear Pit *20*, **77**
Dugdale, Michael 17

Eames, Charles 100
Egypt End, Burnham Beeches, Buckinghamshire **62**
Eliot, T.S. 33

Finsbury Borough Council 19, 35, 39
Finsbury Health Centre, London *34–35*, 35–37, **104–07**
Franck, Carl Ludwig *17*, 20
Frink, Elisabeth 134

Fry, Maxwell 18

Genesta Road, London **54–55**
Gestetner, Sigmund 24, 29
Gestetner Factory, London 141
Ginsberg, Jean 14–16, *15*, 24, 80
Greenwich housing, London 22, *23*
Gropius, Walter 18, 33
Gwynne, Patrick 95

Hallfield, London *42, 43*, **122–25**
Harding, Valentine 17, 60, 62
Hastings, Hubert de Cronin 17
Heath Drive, Gidea Park, Essex **56**
Highpoint I, London 19, 24–29, *25–27*, 35, 40, **84–91**
Highpoint II, London 19, *28–32*, 29–33, 40, **92–103**
Hillfield, Whipsnade, Buckinghamshire 22–24, *23*, **58**
Hitchcock, Henry Russell 29
Holford Square, London 42, 119, 141
Holly Frindle, Whipsnade Park, Bedfordshire 22–24, *23*, **59**

Iofan, Boris 16

Jellicoe, Sir Geoffrey 88, 103
Jordan, Robert Furneaux 96
Joyce, James 33

Katial, Dr Chuni 35

Lakeview, London *47*, **132–33**
Lamb, Michael 98
Lasdun, Denys *17*, 43, 123, 132
Le Corbusier 13, 14, 24, 27, 29, 46, 47, 80, 86, 91, 96
  Ronchamp 29
  Unité d'Habitation, Marseille 29
  Villa Savoye, Poissy 29, 80
Léger, Fernand 33
Lenin Memorial, London *39*, 119, 141
London County Council 130
London Zoo *7*, 19, *19–21*, **66–71**, 141
  Elephant and Rhino Pavilion *20*
  Gorilla House *19*, **66**
  North Gate Kiosk 21, **67**
  Penguin Pool *7*, 19–21, *19, 20*, 31, **68–71**
  Studio of Animal Art *21*, 141
Lubetkin, Drake & Tecton 69–73
Lubetkin, Margaret (née Church) *17*, 32, *38*, 50

MacAlister, Sir Ian 17
Marinetti, Filippo Tommaso 33
Melnikov, Konstantin 13
Mendelsohn, Erich 18
Meyer, Hannes 33
Modern Architectural ReSearch (MARS) Group 33
Moro, Peter 18, 93
Murray, Eileen, *17*
New Delhi 46

Ocean Terminal Building, Karachi *46*

Pajot, Emile 33
Palace of Soviets competition 16–17, *16*

Paris airport project *14*
Peabody Trust 113
Penguin Pool, London Zoo *see* London Zoo
Perret, Auguste 13, 96
Peterlee New Town 42–46, *43, 45, 46*, 50
Picasso, Pablo 33
Pilichowski, A.V. 18, *23*, 55
Pollock, Benjamin 100
Priory Green, London *42*, **112–13**
Priory Heights, London **114–17**
Proust, Marcel 33

Reilly, Charles 17
Richard Rogers Partnership 59
Riley, Harold 35
Royal Institute of British Architects 50

Sadler Street housing project, London 37, *39*
St Andrew's Ambulance Association, Glasgow **137**
Samuel, Godfrey 17, 18–19, 24, 35
Samuely, Felix 19
Schuberski, Prascovia 17
Shaw, George Bernard 17
Sigalin, G. *16*
Sivill House, London *46, 47*, **130–31**
Six Pillars, London **60–61**
Skinner, Francis *17*, 33, 37, 43, 46, 119
Skinner & Bailey 136
Skinner, Bailey & Lubetkin *46*, 113–20, 126–35, 136–37
Skinner & Lubetkin 108
Skinner & Tecton 56
Spa Green, London 39–42, *41*, **108–11**
Stravinsky, Igor 33
Sunnywood Drive, Haywards Heath, West Sussex **64–65**
SVOMAS Studios, St Petersburg 11

Tabard Garden Estate, London **136**
Tecton 17–22, *17*, 33–38, *33*, 43

Upper Kilcott Farm, Gloucestershire *38*
USSR Trades Demountable Exhibition Pavilion 14, *15*, 140
Venesta Display Stand 140
Vkhutemas, Moscow 11
Volodko, J. *14*

West Grove, London **63**
Whipsnade Park, Bedfordshire *20, 21*, **72–73**, 140
  Elephant House *20, 21*, **72**
  Entrance Shelter and Kiosk *20, 21*
  Giraffe House *21*, 140
  Restaurant **73**
  Shelter 140
The Wilderness, Holmbury St Mary **64**
Winter, John 60

Yardeni, Erez 98
Yates, Peter 119
Yorke, F.R.S. 18